SHOPIFY: GENERATING TRAFFIC AND INCREASING SALES

I0416146

BY
HENRY E. PARKINS

COPYRIGHT PAGE

TABLE OF CONTENTS

INTRODUCTION

In the vast digital landscape of ecommerce, establishing a successful online store goes beyond merely launching a website. In today's competitive environment, generating traffic and increasing sales are the lifeblood of any Shopify business. Welcome to "Shopify: Generating Traffic and Increasing Sales," a comprehensive guide designed to equip you with the strategies and techniques necessary to thrive in the dynamic world of online retail.

As the ecommerce industry continues to evolve rapidly, Shopify has emerged as a leading platform, empowering entrepreneurs and businesses of all sizes to create, customize, and manage their online stores with ease. However, with millions of online stores vying for consumer attention, the challenge lies in standing out from the crowd and driving meaningful traffic that converts into sales.

This book is your roadmap to success, offering actionable insights and practical advice on how to optimize your Shopify store, attract the right audience, and ultimately increase your sales revenue.

8

Whether you're a seasoned ecommerce veteran or a newcomer looking to establish your digital presence, this guide is designed to meet you at every stage of your journey.

Throughout the pages of this book, you will discover the fundamental principles of audience targeting, website optimization, content marketing, social media strategies, search engine marketing, analytics utilization, customer relationship building, and business scaling. Each chapter is meticulously crafted to provide you with the knowledge and tools needed to navigate the complexities of online retail and emerge victorious in the competitive marketplace.

As you embark on this transformative journey, remember that success in ecommerce is not merely about the products you sell, but also about the relationships you build, the experiences you create, and the value you deliver to your customers. By implementing the strategies outlined in this book, you will not only drive traffic and increase sales but also foster long-term growth and sustainability for your Shopify business.

So, let us embark on this exhilarating adventure together, as we unlock the secrets to success in the digital realm and empower you to achieve your loftiest ecommerce ambitions. The journey ahead may be challenging, but with dedication, perseverance, and the guidance found within these pages, the possibilities for your Shopify business are limitless.

Brief Overview of the Shopify Platform

Shopify stands as a beacon in the ever-expanding universe of ecommerce platforms, offering entrepreneurs and businesses a robust and intuitive solution to create, manage, and scale their online stores with unparalleled ease and efficiency. Founded in 2006, Shopify has evolved into a powerhouse, powering over a million businesses worldwide and facilitating billions of dollars in online transactions annually.

At its core, Shopify provides a comprehensive suite of tools and features designed to streamline the entire ecommerce process, from storefront creation and product management to payment processing and order fulfillment. With its user-friendly interface and customizable themes, Shopify empowers users to design visually stunning and mobile-responsive websites that reflect their brand identity and resonate with their target audience.

One of Shopify's defining features is its scalability, allowing businesses of all sizes to start small and grow exponentially without the constraints of traditional brick-and-mortar establishments. Whether you're a budding entrepreneur launching your first online venture or an established brand seeking to expand your digital footprint, Shopify offers flexible pricing plans and powerful integrations to accommodate your evolving needs and ambitions.

Moreover, Shopify's extensive app marketplace provides access to a wealth of third-party applications and plugins, allowing users to enhance their store's functionality and optimize their operations. From marketing automation and customer relationship management to inventory management and analytics, the possibilities are endless, enabling Shopify merchants to stay ahead of the curve and remain competitive in a rapidly changing landscape.

In addition to its robust feature set, Shopify places a strong emphasis on security and reliability, ensuring that merchants and their customers can transact with confidence and peace of mind. With industry-leading encryption protocols and PCI compliance, Shopify provides a secure environment for sensitive data and financial transactions, safeguarding against potential threats and vulnerabilities.

In essence, Shopify represents more than just a platform it's a catalyst for innovation, empowerment, and entrepreneurship. By democratizing access to ecommerce tools and resources, Shopify empowers individuals and businesses to turn their dreams into reality and redefine the future of retail in the digital age.

Importance of Generating Traffic and Increasing Sales for Shopify Businesses

In the bustling realm of ecommerce, where millions of online stores vie for consumer attention, the ability to generate traffic and increase sales is paramount to the success and sustainability of Shopify businesses. While Shopify provides a powerful platform for creating and managing online stores, its true potential is unlocked only when coupled with effective marketing strategies and sales optimization techniques.

Visibility and Brand Awareness:
Generating traffic is the gateway to visibility and brand awareness in the crowded digital marketplace. Without a steady stream of visitors to your Shopify store, your products and offerings remain hidden from potential customers. By increasing traffic through targeted marketing efforts and strategic promotions, Shopify businesses can expand their reach and attract new audiences, ultimately strengthening brand recognition and market presence.

Revenue Growth and Profitability: Sales are the lifeblood of any business, and Shopify is no exception. Increasing sales revenue directly contributes to the financial health and

13

profitability of Shopify businesses, enabling them to reinvest in growth initiatives, expand product offerings, and improve customer experiences. By implementing effective sales optimization strategies, such as upselling, cross-selling, and promotional campaigns, Shopify merchants can maximize revenue potential and achieve sustainable growth over time.

Competitive Edge and Market Differentiation:
In a competitive landscape where consumers are spoiled for choice, generating traffic and increasing sales can provide Shopify businesses with a distinct competitive edge. By delivering exceptional value propositions, personalized shopping experiences, and superior customer service, Shopify merchants can differentiate themselves from competitors and carve out a unique niche in the market. This differentiation not only attracts loyal customers but also fosters long-term brand loyalty and advocacy, driving sustained success and market leadership.

Data-driven Insights and Continuous Improvement:

Generating traffic and increasing sales on Shopify provide valuable insights into customer behavior, preferences, and trends. By analyzing metrics such as website traffic, conversion rates, and sales performance, Shopify merchants can gain actionable insights that inform strategic decision-making and drive continuous improvement. Through A/B testing, experimentation, and data-driven optimization, Shopify businesses can refine their marketing efforts, enhance user experiences, and stay ahead of evolving consumer demands, ensuring long-term relevance and competitiveness in the marketplace.

In summary, the importance of generating traffic and increasing sales for Shopify businesses cannot be overstated. By prioritizing visibility, revenue growth, market differentiation, and data-driven optimization, Shopify merchants can unlock the full potential of the platform, achieve their business objectives, and thrive in the dynamic world of ecommerce. As we journey through the pages of this book, we will explore proven strategies and best practices for generating traffic and increasing sales on Shopify, empowering you to unleash the full potential of your online store and achieve unparalleled success in the digital marketplace.

Purpose and Scope of the Book: "Shopify: Generating Traffic and Increasing Sales"

Purpose: The purpose of "Shopify: Generating Traffic and Increasing Sales" is to serve as a comprehensive guide and strategic resource for Shopify merchants seeking to maximize their online store's potential. In a digital landscape characterized by fierce competition and evolving consumer behaviors, the book aims to equip Shopify entrepreneurs with the knowledge, tools, and techniques needed to drive meaningful traffic, increase sales revenue, and achieve sustainable growth in the dynamic world of ecommerce.

Scope:

Strategic Frameworks: The book provides a strategic framework for understanding the nuances of generating traffic and increasing sales on the Shopify platform. It covers essential concepts such

16

as audience targeting, website optimization, content marketing, social media strategies, search engine marketing, analytics utilization, customer relationship building, and business scaling.

Practical Guidance: Each chapter offers practical guidance, actionable insights, and best practices drawn from real-world examples and industry expertise. Readers will learn how to apply proven strategies and techniques to their Shopify businesses, leveraging the platform's capabilities to achieve tangible results and competitive advantage.

Comprehensive Coverage: From beginner-friendly tips to advanced strategies, the book caters to Shopify merchants at every stage of their journey, whether they're launching their first online store or looking to scale their existing business. It covers a wide range of topics, including website design, product optimization, marketing channels, analytics interpretation, customer retention, and business expansion.

Adaptability and Innovation: Recognizing the ever-evolving nature of

ecommerce, the book emphasizes the importance of adaptability and innovation in navigating the complexities of the digital marketplace. It encourages readers to stay informed about emerging trends, experiment with new technologies, and iterate on their strategies to stay ahead of the curve and remain competitive in a rapidly changing landscape.

Empowerment and Success:

Ultimately, the book aims to empower Shopify merchants to unlock their full potential and achieve unparalleled success in their ecommerce endeavors. By providing actionable advice, practical tools, and strategic frameworks, it equips readers with the confidence and capabilities needed to overcome challenges, seize opportunities, and realize their loftiest business aspirations on the Shopify platform.

In summary, "Shopify: Generating Traffic and Increasing Sales" is more than just a guidebook it's a roadmap to success in the digital realm, offering a holistic approach to driving traffic, increasing sales, and building thriving Shopify businesses in an increasingly competitive marketplace.

Through its purpose-driven content and comprehensive scope, the book aims to inspire, educate, and empower entrepreneurs to harness the full potential of Shopify and unlock new opportunities for growth and prosperity.

CHAPTER 1

UNDERSTANDING YOUR AUDIENCE

One of the foundational pillars of successful ecommerce lies in understanding your audience. In the digital realm, where competition is fierce and consumer preferences are ever-evolving, knowing who your customers are and what drives their purchasing decisions is essential for generating traffic and increasing sales on your Shopify store.

Identifying Target Market and Demographics: The first step in understanding your audience is identifying your target market and demographics. Who are the people most likely to be interested in your products or services? What are their demographics, including age, gender, location, income level, and interests? By conducting thorough market research and demographic analysis, you can gain valuable insights into the characteristics and preferences of your target audience.

Conducting Market Research and Competitor Analysis: Market research and competitor analysis play a crucial role in understanding your audience. What are the current trends and preferences in your industry? Who are your competitors, and what strategies are they employing to attract customers? By analyzing market trends, consumer behavior, and competitor offerings, you can identify gaps, opportunities, and areas for differentiation in the marketplace.

Creating Buyer Personas: Buyer personas are fictional representations of your ideal customers, based on real data and insights. By creating detailed buyer personas, including demographic information, pain points, goals, and purchasing behaviors, you can better understand the motivations and needs of your target audience. This allows you to tailor your marketing messages, product offerings, and user experiences to resonate with specific customer segments.

Understanding Customer Journey and Behavior: Understanding the customer journey and behavior is critical for optimizing your Shopify store and driving conversions. How do customers discover your store? What actions do they take before making a purchase? By mapping out the customer journey and analyzing user behavior through tools like Google Analytics, you can identify touchpoints, pain points, and opportunities to optimize the user experience and increase sales.

Leveraging Customer Feedback and Insights: Customer feedback and insights are invaluable sources of information for understanding your audience. Whether through surveys, reviews, or social media interactions, listening to your customers' feedback can provide valuable insights into their preferences, concerns, and expectations. By actively soliciting and responding to customer feedback, you can demonstrate your commitment to customer satisfaction and continuously improve your products and services.

Identifying Target Market and Demographics

Identifying your target market and demographics is the cornerstone of effective marketing and sales strategies on Shopify. Your target market represents the specific group of consumers who are most likely to be interested in your products or services. By understanding their demographics, behaviors, and preferences, you can tailor your marketing efforts to reach the right audience and drive meaningful traffic to your Shopify store.

Demographic Factors:

Age: Determine the age range of your target audience. Are your products geared towards teenagers, young adults, middle-aged individuals, or seniors?

Gender: Consider the gender breakdown of your target market. Are your products more appealing to males, females, or both?

Location: Understand the geographical location of your target audience. Are they located in specific regions, countries, or urban vs. rural areas?

Income Level: Consider the income level of your target market. Are they high-income earners, middle-class consumers, or budget-conscious individuals?

Education Level: Determine the education level of your target audience. Are they college-educated professionals, high school graduates, or individuals with specialized skills?

Psychographic Factors:

Lifestyle: Consider the lifestyle choices and values of your target market. Are they health-conscious, environmentally conscious, or tech-savvy?

Interests: Identify the hobbies, interests, and passions of your target audience. What activities do they enjoy, and what are their leisure pursuits?

Values: Understand the values and beliefs that resonate with your target market. What causes or social issues are important to them?

Personality Traits: Consider the personality traits and characteristics of your target audience. Are they adventurous, introverted, extroverted, or family-oriented?

Behavioral Factors:

Buying Behavior: Analyze the purchasing behavior of your target market. How often do they make purchases, and what factors influence their buying decisions?

Online Behavior: Understand the online behavior and preferences of your target audience. How do they prefer to shop online, and which digital channels do they frequent?

Brand Affinity: Identify the brands and products that resonate with your target market. What are their brand preferences, and what influences their brand loyalty?

Media Consumption: Determine the media consumption habits of your target audience. Which platforms do they use for information, entertainment, and social interaction?

Conducting Market Research and Competitor Analysis

Market research and competitor analysis are integral components of any successful ecommerce strategy on Shopify. By understanding market trends, consumer preferences, and competitor strategies, you can identify opportunities, mitigate risks, and make informed decisions to drive traffic and increase sales on your Shopify store.

Identifying Market Trends:

Monitor industry trends, emerging technologies, and shifting consumer behaviors relevant to your niche.

Stay updated on market reports, industry publications, and credible sources of market intelligence.

Identify patterns, preferences, and changes in consumer demand that may impact your Shopify business.

Understanding Consumer Preferences:

Conduct surveys, interviews, and focus groups to gather insights into consumer preferences, needs, and pain points.

Analyze customer feedback, reviews, and social media interactions to understand sentiment and sentiment.

Identify key drivers of consumer behavior, such as price sensitivity, product quality, and brand perception.

Assessing Market Size and Growth Potential:

Estimate the size and growth potential of your target market by analyzing demographic data, market segmentation, and consumer spending patterns.

Evaluate market saturation, competitive intensity, and barriers to entry within your industry.

Identify niche markets, underserved segments, and untapped opportunities for expansion.

Analyzing Competitor Strategies:

Identify direct and indirect competitors operating in your industry or niche.

Analyze competitor websites, product offerings, pricing strategies, and promotional tactics.

Identify strengths, weaknesses, opportunities, and threats (SWOT analysis) for each competitor.

Benchmark your Shopify store against competitors to identify areas for improvement and differentiation.

Monitoring Industry Benchmarks and Best Practices:

Monitor industry benchmarks, key performance indicators (KPIs), and best practices for ecommerce success.

Analyze industry leaders and successful Shopify stores to identify trends, strategies, and tactics worth emulating.

Stay abreast of technological advancements, regulatory changes, and disruptive innovations that may impact your industry.

28

Gathering Customer Insights and Feedback:

Leverage customer data, purchase history, and behavioral analytics to gain insights into customer preferences and buying patterns.

Solicit feedback through surveys, reviews, and customer support interactions to identify areas for improvement and innovation.

Engage with customers on social media platforms, online forums, and community groups to foster relationships and gather insights.

Creating Buyer Personas

Buyer personas are fictional representations of your ideal customers, based on real data and insights. Developing detailed buyer personas is essential for understanding the motivations, needs, and preferences of your target audience on Shopify. By crafting comprehensive buyer personas, you can tailor your marketing efforts, product offerings, and user experiences to resonate with specific customer segments and drive traffic and sales to your Shopify store.

29

Gather Data and Insights:

Collect demographic information, including age, gender, location, income level, education level, and occupation, through surveys, analytics, and customer databases.

Gather psychographic data, such as lifestyle choices, interests, values, hobbies, and personality traits, through customer interviews, focus groups, and social media interactions.

Analyze behavioral data, including purchasing behavior, online preferences, device usage, and brand affinity, through website analytics, purchase history, and customer feedback.

Identify Common Patterns and Trends:

Look for common patterns and trends among your target audience, including shared preferences, pain points, goals, and behaviors.

Identify recurring themes and insights that can help you segment your audience into distinct buyer personas based on similarities and differences.

30

Develop Persona Profiles:

Create individual persona profiles for each segment of your target audience, incorporating demographic, psychographic, and behavioral insights.

Give each persona a name, photo, and descriptive characteristics to bring them to life and make them relatable to your team.

Include details such as age, gender, occupation, income level, family status, hobbies, interests, values, goals, challenges, and preferred communication channels.

Validate and Refine Personas:

Validate your personas by testing them against real-world data and customer feedback to ensure accuracy and relevance.

Refine your personas over time based on new insights, changing market dynamics, and evolving customer preferences.

Continuously update and iterate on your personas to keep them aligned with the needs and expectations of your target audience.

31

Use Personas to Inform Marketing Strategies:

Tailor your marketing messages, content, and promotions to resonate with the unique needs and preferences of each persona.

Customize your product offerings, features, and pricing strategies to address the specific pain points and goals of each persona.

Select appropriate marketing channels and tactics based on the preferred communication channels and online behaviors of each persona.

By creating detailed buyer personas, you can gain a deeper understanding of your target audience and effectively tailor your marketing strategies to drive traffic and increase sales on your Shopify store. Personas serve as invaluable tools for aligning your efforts with the needs and preferences of your customers, ultimately helping you build meaningful relationships and drive sustainable growth in the competitive ecommerce landscape.

CHAPTER 2

OPTIMIZING PRODUCT LISTINGS FOR SEARCH ENGINES (SEO)

Search engine optimization (SEO) plays a crucial role in driving organic traffic to your Shopify store and increasing visibility in search engine results pages (SERPs). By optimizing your product listings for SEO, you can improve your store's chances of being discovered by potential customers who are actively searching for products like yours. Here are key strategies to optimize product listings for SEO:

Keyword Research

Conduct thorough keyword research to identify relevant search terms and phrases that your target audience is using.

Use keyword research tools like Google Keyword Planner, SEMrush, or Ahrefs to discover high-volume and low-competition keywords related to your products.

Consider long-tail keywords and semantic variations to capture specific search intent and target niche audiences.

Optimize Product Titles

Include primary keywords at the beginning of product titles to improve relevance and visibility.

Keep titles descriptive, concise, and easy to understand, while accurately representing the product.

Incorporate unique selling points, brand names, and relevant attributes to differentiate your products in search results.

Craft Compelling Meta Descriptions

Write compelling meta descriptions that entice users to click through to your product pages.

Include primary keywords and persuasive language to highlight key features, benefits, and value propositions.

Keep meta descriptions under 160 characters to ensure they display fully in search engine results.

Optimize Product Descriptions

Write unique, detailed, and informative product descriptions that accurately describe the features, benefits, and specifications of each product.

Incorporate relevant keywords naturally throughout the product description, but avoid keyword stuffing or unnatural keyword placement.

Use bullet points, headings, and formatting to improve readability and scanability for both users and search engines.

Utilize Alt Text for Images:

Optimize image alt text with descriptive keywords to improve accessibility and help search engines understand the content of your images.

Use descriptive and relevant alt text that accurately describes the image and its context within the product listing.

Avoid generic or repetitive alt text and instead provide specific details that enhance the user experience.

Optimize URL Structure:

35

Create clean, descriptive, and SEO-friendly URLs for each product page, incorporating relevant keywords and avoiding unnecessary parameters or symbols.

Use hyphens to separate words in URLs and keep them concise and easy to read.

Avoid using generic or auto-generated URLs that lack descriptive information and context.

Optimize Product Tags and Categories

Use relevant tags and categories to organize your products and improve navigation within your Shopify store.

Incorporate keywords into product tags and categories to enhance discoverability and improve internal linking structure.

Keep product tags and categories consistent, logical, and user-friendly to facilitate a seamless browsing experience.

By implementing these SEO strategies and best practices, you can optimize your Shopify product listings to rank higher in search engine results, attract organic traffic, and increase visibility to potential customers. Continuously monitor performance metrics, track keyword rankings, and refine your optimization efforts to stay competitive and drive sustained traffic and sales growth.

Enhancing the Customer Experience with Responsive Design

In the ever-evolving landscape of ecommerce, providing a seamless and engaging user experience across all devices is paramount to the success of your Shopify store. Responsive design is a fundamental aspect of creating a website that adapts fluidly to various screen sizes and devices, ensuring that customers can easily navigate, engage, and transact with your brand. Here's how you can enhance the customer experience with responsive design on Shopify:

Adaptability Across Devices

Responsive design enables your Shopify store to automatically adjust its layout, content, and functionality based on the user's device, whether it's a desktop, laptop, tablet, or smartphone.

37

Ensure that your website's design elements, including images, text, buttons, and navigation menus, scale proportionally and maintain optimal visibility and usability across all devices.

Improved Usability and Navigation

Prioritize user-friendly navigation and intuitive layouts that allow customers to easily find products, browse categories, and access important information regardless of the device they're using.

Implement clear and accessible navigation menus, collapsible sections, and breadcrumb trails to help users navigate your Shopify store seamlessly and efficiently.

Optimized Load Times and Performance

Optimize page load times and performance by minimizing unnecessary elements, compressing images, and leveraging browser caching to ensure a smooth and responsive browsing experience for users on all devices.

Monitor website performance metrics and address any issues related to slow loading times, unresponsive elements, or usability errors that may impact the customer experience.

Consistent Branding and Visual Identity

Maintain consistent branding and visual identity across all devices, ensuring that your Shopify store reflects your brand's personality, values, and aesthetics consistently.

Use responsive design techniques to adapt brand elements, such as logos, colors, fonts, and imagery, to different screen sizes and resolutions without compromising visual integrity or brand recognition.

Mobile-Friendly Checkout Process

Streamline the checkout process for mobile users by optimizing form fields, reducing unnecessary steps, and minimizing friction points that may hinder conversion rates.

39

Implement mobile-friendly payment options, autofill capabilities, and guest checkout functionality to simplify the purchasing experience and increase customer satisfaction.

Enhanced User Engagement and Interactivity

Leverage responsive design to create interactive and engaging experiences that captivate users and encourage interaction with your Shopify store.

Incorporate dynamic elements, such as carousels, sliders, accordions, and product galleries, that respond seamlessly to user interactions and gestures on touch-enabled devices.

Continuous Testing and Optimization

Regularly test your Shopify store across various devices, browsers, and operating systems to identify any responsiveness issues or inconsistencies that may arise.

Use tools like Google's Mobile-Friendly Test and browser developer tools to diagnose and address responsive design issues effectively.

Collect feedback from users, monitor analytics data, and iterate on your responsive design strategy to continuously improve the customer experience and drive conversions.

By prioritizing responsive design principles and optimizing your Shopify store for seamless cross-device compatibility, you can create a cohesive and engaging user experience that delights customers and drives sales. Responsive design is not only a best practice—it's a fundamental component of modern ecommerce that enables you to connect with customers wherever they are and on whatever device they're using, ultimately contributing to the success and growth of your Shopify business.

Implementing Effective Product Categorization and Navigation

Organizing your products effectively and providing intuitive navigation are essential components of creating a user-friendly and conversion-focused Shopify store. By implementing strategic product categorization and navigation techniques, you can enhance the browsing experience for your customers, help them discover relevant products easily, and ultimately increase sales. Here's how to implement effective product categorization and navigation on Shopify:

Understand Your Product Range

Begin by understanding the breadth and depth of your product offerings. Identify the main categories and subcategories that best represent your products and align with your customers' needs and preferences.

Create Clear and Logical Categories

Organize your products into clear and logical categories that reflect their characteristics, features, and use cases. Use broad categories to encompass a range of related products and subcategories to provide more specific groupings.

Use Descriptive Category Names

Choose descriptive and easy-to-understand category names that clearly communicate the contents of each section. Avoid using industry-specific jargon or ambiguous terms that may confuse customers.

Implement Hierarchical Navigation

Implement a hierarchical navigation structure that allows customers to navigate through your Shopify store intuitively. Use dropdown menus, expandable categories, and breadcrumb trails to guide users through different levels of your product hierarchy.

Prioritize User-Friendly Navigation Menus

Design navigation menus that are easy to access, visually appealing, and responsive across all devices. Use clear labels, consistent formatting, and logical hierarchies to help users navigate your store effortlessly.

Facilitate Search and Filtering Options

Provide search functionality with autocomplete suggestions and advanced filtering options to help users find specific products quickly. Allow users to filter products by attributes such as price, size, color, brand, and availability to refine their search results.

Promote Featured and Best-Selling Products

Highlight featured and best-selling products prominently within your navigation menus and category pages to attract attention and encourage exploration. Use banners, badges, and promotional labels to showcase special offers, new arrivals, and seasonal collections.

Optimize Product Page Structure

Standardize the layout and structure of your product pages to ensure consistency and clarity across your Shopify store. Place key product information, including images, descriptions, pricing, and availability, in easily accessible locations to streamline the shopping experience.

Enable Quick View and Product Previews

Implement quick view functionality and product previews that allow users to preview product details, images, and pricing without leaving the category page. This reduces friction and enables users to make informed decisions more efficiently.

Monitor and Iterate Based on User Feedback

Monitor user behavior, engagement metrics, and conversion rates to identify any pain points or usability issues related to product categorization and navigation.

Solicit feedback from customers through surveys, user testing, and analytics to understand their preferences and challenges. Use this feedback to iterate and refine your navigation structure and product categorization strategy over time.

By implementing these effective product categorization and navigation strategies, you can create a seamless and intuitive browsing experience for your customers on Shopify. By making it easy for users to explore your product offerings, find relevant items, and make informed

45

purchase decisions, you can increase engagement, drive traffic, and ultimately boost sales on your Shopify store.

CHAPTER 3

CONTENT MARKETING STRATEGIES

Content marketing is a powerful strategy for driving traffic, increasing brand awareness, and ultimately boosting sales on your Shopify store. By creating valuable, relevant, and engaging content, you can attract and engage your target audience, establish credibility and authority in your niche, and nurture relationships with potential customers. Here are key content marketing strategies to implement for generating traffic and increasing sales on Shopify:

Blog Posts and Articles

Create a blog on your Shopify store and regularly publish informative and engaging articles related to your industry, products, and target audience's interests.

Address common pain points, provide solutions to customer problems, and offer valuable insights and tips that demonstrate your expertise and build trust with your audience.

47

Optimize blog posts for search engines by incorporating relevant keywords, internal links, and meta tags to improve visibility and attract organic traffic.

Product Guides and Tutorials

Develop comprehensive product guides, tutorials, and how-to articles that educate customers about your products, showcase their features and benefits, and provide practical tips for using them effectively.

Use multimedia elements such as videos, images, and infographics to enhance the visual appeal and effectiveness of your product guides and tutorials.

Share real-life examples, case studies, and customer testimonials to illustrate the value and versatility of your products in action.

Email Marketing Campaigns:

Build an email list of subscribers and regularly send out newsletters, promotional offers, and product updates to keep customers engaged and informed.

Personalize email content based on customer preferences, purchase history, and browsing behavior to deliver relevant and targeted messaging that resonates with each recipient.

Use compelling subject lines, clear calls-to-action, and visually appealing design to encourage opens, clicks, and conversions.

Social Media Content:

Leverage social media platforms such as Facebook, Instagram, Twitter, and Pinterest to share engaging content, interact with followers, and drive traffic to your Shopify store.

Create visually appealing graphics, videos, and carousel ads that showcase your products, highlight special promotions, and encourage user engagement.

Encourage user-generated content by hosting contests, featuring customer testimonials, and sharing user-generated photos and videos that showcase your products in real-life scenarios.

Ebooks and Whitepapers:

Develop in-depth ebooks, whitepapers, and downloadable resources that offer valuable insights, research findings, and industry trends related to your niche.

Gate premium content behind lead capture forms to capture email addresses and expand your subscriber base. Provide a sneak peek or summary of the content to entice users to download the full resource.

Promote ebooks and whitepapers through blog posts, social media, and email marketing campaigns to maximize reach and engagement.

Podcasts and Webinars:

Host podcasts and webinars featuring industry experts, thought leaders, and influencers to discuss relevant topics, share insights, and provide actionable advice to your audience.

Invite guest speakers, conduct interviews, and encourage audience participation to foster engagement and build a sense of community around your brand.

Repurpose podcast episodes and webinar recordings into blog posts, social media snippets, and email newsletters to extend their reach and provide ongoing value to your audience.

User-Generated Content Campaigns:

Encourage customers to create and share user-generated content such as reviews, testimonials, unboxing videos, and product photos on social media and other digital platforms.

Showcase user-generated content on your Shopify store, social media profiles, and marketing materials to build social proof, foster trust, and inspire confidence in your products.

Express gratitude to customers for their contributions and incentivize participation with rewards, discounts, or exclusive offers to encourage ongoing engagement and advocacy.

Creating Compelling Product Descriptions and Visuals

In the competitive landscape of ecommerce, compelling product descriptions and visuals are essential for capturing the attention of potential customers, conveying the value proposition of your products, and ultimately driving sales on your Shopify store. Here's how to

51

create compelling product descriptions and visuals that resonate with your target audience and inspire action:

Understand Your Target Audience:

Before crafting product descriptions and visuals, take the time to understand your target audience's needs, preferences, and pain points.

Tailor your messaging and imagery to resonate with the interests, aspirations, and lifestyle of your ideal customers.

Highlight Key Features and Benefits:

Clearly articulate the key features and benefits of your products in your descriptions, focusing on how they solve problems or fulfill needs for your customers.

Use persuasive language and storytelling techniques to create an emotional connection with your audience and demonstrate the value proposition of your products.

Use Descriptive and Engaging Language:

Choose descriptive and evocative language that paints a vivid picture of the product and its benefits in the mind of the customer.

Incorporate sensory details and emotional triggers to appeal to the senses and evoke an emotional response from your audience.

Optimize for Search Engines:

Incorporate relevant keywords and phrases into your product descriptions to improve search engine visibility and attract organic traffic to your Shopify store.

Use natural language and avoid keyword stuffing to ensure that your descriptions read smoothly and provide value to human readers.

Format for Readability:

Break up text into short paragraphs, bullet points, and headings to improve readability and scanability for users browsing your product pages.

Use formatting elements such as bold text, italics, and color accents to highlight important information and draw attention to key selling points.

Tell a Story with Visuals:

Invest in high-quality product photography and visual assets that showcase your products in the best possible light.

Use a variety of images, including close-ups, lifestyle shots, and product demonstrations, to provide different perspectives and contexts for your products.

Incorporate user-generated content, such as customer photos and videos, to add authenticity and social proof to your product pages.

Optimize Image Quality and Size:

Ensure that product images are clear, crisp, and high-resolution, with accurate colors and details that accurately represent the product.

Optimize image file sizes to reduce load times and improve page performance without sacrificing image quality or resolution.

Provide Detailed Product Information:

Include detailed specifications, dimensions, materials, and care instructions in your product descriptions to help customers make informed purchasing decisions.

Anticipate and address common questions and concerns that customers may have about the product, such as sizing, compatibility, and warranty information.

Create a Consistent Brand Voice:

Develop a consistent brand voice and tone that reflects your brand's personality, values, and identity across all product descriptions and visuals.

Use language and imagery that align with your brand's positioning and resonate with your target audience's preferences and expectations.

Test and Iterate Based on Feedback:

Continuously monitor customer feedback, engagement metrics, and conversion rates to evaluate the effectiveness of your product descriptions and visuals.

A/B test different variations of product descriptions, imagery, and calls-to-action to identify what resonates best with your audience and drives the highest levels of engagement and conversion.

Blogging and Content Creation to Drive Traffic

In the dynamic world of ecommerce, blogging and content creation serve as powerful tools for driving traffic, increasing brand visibility, and ultimately boosting sales on your Shopify store. By consistently producing valuable, relevant, and engaging content, you can attract and retain the attention of your target audience, establish your authority in your niche, and cultivate meaningful relationships with potential customers. Here's how to leverage blogging and content creation effectively to drive traffic for your Shopify store:

Identify Your Target Audience and Content Goals:

Start by understanding your target audience's demographics, interests,

56

preferences, and pain points. Identify the topics, themes, and formats that resonate most with your audience and align with your brand's goals and values.

Develop a Content Strategy:

Define clear objectives and goals for your content marketing efforts, such as increasing website traffic, generating leads, or driving product sales.

Conduct keyword research and competitive analysis to identify relevant topics, keywords, and content gaps that present opportunities for your Shopify store.

Create a content calendar outlining your publishing schedule, topics, formats, and distribution channels to maintain consistency and accountability.

Create Valuable and Engaging Content:

Produce high-quality, informative, and engaging content that provides value to your audience and addresses their needs, interests, and pain points.

Experiment with different content formats, including blog posts, articles, infographics, videos, podcasts, and downloadable

57

resources, to cater to diverse audience preferences and consumption habits.

Incorporate storytelling techniques, real-life examples, case studies, and expert insights to make your content relatable, authentic, and memorable.

Optimize Content for Search Engines:

Conduct keyword research to identify relevant keywords and phrases that your target audience is searching for.

Optimize your content for search engines by incorporating target keywords naturally into your titles, headings, meta descriptions, and body copy.

Use descriptive alt text, file names, and captions for images and multimedia content to improve accessibility and search engine visibility.

Promote Content Across Channels:

Share your content across multiple channels and platforms to maximize reach and engagement. Leverage social media, email marketing, influencer partnerships, and online communities to amplify your content's visibility and impact.

Encourage social sharing and engagement by including social sharing buttons, calls-to-action, and interactive elements within your content.

Collaborate with industry influencers, thought leaders, and content creators to expand your audience reach and tap into new networks and communities.

Encourage User Engagement and Feedback:

Foster meaningful conversations and interactions with your audience by encouraging comments, questions, and feedback on your blog posts and content assets.

Respond promptly to user comments, address customer inquiries, and acknowledge user-generated content to demonstrate your commitment to customer engagement and satisfaction.

Use feedback and insights from your audience to inform future content creation efforts, identify emerging trends, and refine your content strategy over time.

Measure and Analyze Performance Metrics:

Monitor key performance indicators (KPIs) such as website traffic, page views, bounce rates, time on page, social shares, and conversion rates to assess the effectiveness of your content marketing efforts.

Use web analytics tools, content management systems (CMS), and social media analytics platforms to track and analyze audience behavior, content engagement, and traffic sources.

Identify trends, patterns, and opportunities for optimization based on data-driven insights and performance metrics, and adjust your content strategy accordingly.

Leveraging User-Generated Content and Testimonials

User-generated content (UGC) and testimonials are powerful assets that can significantly impact the success of your Shopify store by building trust, credibility, and authenticity among potential customers. By showcasing real-life experiences and opinions from satisfied customers, you can inspire confidence in your products, foster community engagement, and ultimately drive traffic and increase sales. Here's how to effectively leverage user-generated content and testimonials on your Shopify store:

Encourage Customer Reviews and Ratings:

Prompt customers to leave reviews and ratings for products they've purchased from your Shopify store. Make the review process simple and accessible, and consider offering incentives or rewards for leaving feedback.

Display product reviews and ratings prominently on your product pages to provide social proof and help prospective buyers make informed purchasing decisions.

Respond to customer reviews, both positive and negative, in a timely and professional manner to demonstrate your commitment to customer satisfaction and engagement.

Curate User-Generated Content:

Encourage customers to share their experiences with your products by submitting user-generated content such as photos, videos, testimonials, and product reviews.

Create dedicated sections on your Shopify store to showcase user-generated content, such as customer galleries, testimonials pages, or social media feeds.

Curate and feature user-generated content that highlights the diversity of your customer base and showcases the real-life benefits and applications of your products.

Incorporate Social Proof and Trust Signals:

Highlight positive customer testimonials, endorsements, and success stories prominently throughout your Shopify store to build trust and credibility with prospective buyers.

Use customer testimonials and endorsements in your product descriptions, landing pages, checkout process, and marketing materials to reinforce the value proposition of your products and alleviate purchase hesitations.

Include trust signals such as trust badges, security seals, and industry certifications to reassure customers about the safety, security, and authenticity of their transactions.

Engage with User-Generated Content:

Foster community engagement and participation by actively engaging with user-generated content on social media platforms, review websites, and community forums.

Like, share, and comment on customer-generated posts and reviews to show appreciation for their support and contributions.

Incorporate user-generated content into your social media marketing campaigns, email newsletters, and promotional materials to amplify its reach and impact.

Showcase Customer Testimonials and Case Studies:

Collect and showcase customer testimonials, case studies, and success

63

stories that illustrate the tangible benefits and results achieved by using your products.

Feature testimonials from satisfied customers across different demographics, industries, and use cases to demonstrate the versatility and effectiveness of your products.

Use compelling storytelling techniques and visual elements to bring customer testimonials and case studies to life and make them resonate with your target audience.

Request Permission and Provide Attribution:

Always obtain explicit permission from customers before using their content, testimonials, or reviews for promotional purposes.

Clearly communicate how user-generated content will be used and ensure that customers feel comfortable and confident in sharing their experiences publicly.

Provide proper attribution and acknowledgment to customers whose content and testimonials are featured on your Shopify store, respecting their contributions and privacy rights.

Utilizing Email Marketing Campaigns and Newsletters

Email marketing is a powerful tool for driving traffic, increasing engagement, and boosting sales on your Shopify store. By leveraging email campaigns and newsletters effectively, you can nurture relationships with your audience, deliver targeted messaging, and encourage repeat purchases. Here's how to utilize email marketing campaigns and newsletters to generate traffic and increase sales on Shopify:

Build and Segment Your Email List:

Develop a comprehensive email list by capturing email addresses through website sign-up forms, pop-ups, lead magnets, and checkout opt-ins on your Shopify store.

Segment your email list based on customer demographics, purchase history, engagement level, and preferences to deliver personalized and relevant content to each segment.

65

Create Compelling Email Content:

Craft compelling email content that resonates with your audience and aligns with their interests, preferences, and purchasing behavior.

Use attention-grabbing subject lines, personalized greetings, and clear calls-to-action (CTAs) to entice recipients to open and engage with your emails.

Experiment with different content formats, such as product promotions, educational content, curated collections, and exclusive offers, to keep your emails fresh and engaging.

Segmented Email Campaigns:

Develop targeted email campaigns tailored to specific segments of your audience, such as new subscribers, first-time buyers, loyal customers, and dormant subscribers.

Send personalized product recommendations, relevant content, and exclusive offers based on each segment's preferences, browsing history, and purchase behavior.

Use dynamic content blocks and conditional logic to customize email content dynamically based on recipient data and behavior.

Automate Email Sequences:

Set up automated email sequences and workflows to deliver timely and relevant messages to subscribers at various stages of the customer journey.

Implement welcome series, abandoned cart reminders, post-purchase follow-ups, and re-engagement campaigns to nurture relationships, recover lost sales, and drive customer retention.

Use triggers and conditions to send emails based on specific actions or events, such as website visits, email opens, product views, and purchase activity.

Optimize for Mobile Responsiveness:

Ensure that your email templates and designs are mobile-responsive and optimized for viewing on smartphones and tablets.

Use a responsive email template that adjusts seamlessly to different screen sizes and resolutions to deliver a consistent and user-friendly experience across devices.

Test your email campaigns across various email clients, devices, and operating systems to identify any rendering issues or usability concerns.

Track and Analyze Performance Metrics:

Monitor key performance indicators (KPIs) such as open rates, click-through rates (CTRs), conversion rates, and revenue generated from email campaigns.

Use email analytics and reporting tools to track campaign performance, identify trends, and gain insights into subscriber engagement and behavior.

A/B test different email elements, including subject lines, sender names, CTAs, and content variations, to optimize performance and maximize results.

Provide Value and Encourage Engagement:

Deliver valuable content and offers that provide tangible benefits to your subscribers, such as exclusive discounts,

68

early access to new products, and helpful tips and resources.

Encourage subscriber engagement and interaction through polls, surveys, quizzes, and user-generated content submissions.

Foster a sense of community and belonging by inviting subscribers to join loyalty programs, participate in contests, and share their experiences with your brand.

CHAPTER 4

SOCIAL MEDIA MARKETING

Social media marketing is a powerful tool for driving traffic, increasing brand awareness, and boosting sales on your Shopify store. By leveraging social media platforms effectively, you can reach a broader audience, engage with your target market, and foster meaningful connections with potential customers. Here's how to implement social media marketing strategies to generate traffic and increase sales on Shopify:

Choose the Right Social Media Platforms:

Identify the social media platforms that align best with your target audience, industry, and marketing objectives.

Consider factors such as demographics, user behavior, platform features, and advertising options when selecting the most suitable platforms for your Shopify store.

Develop a Consistent Brand Presence:

Create a cohesive and recognizable brand presence across your social media profiles, including profile pictures, cover photos, bios, and branded content.

Maintain consistency in tone, voice, and visual identity to reinforce your brand messaging and values across all social media channels.

Share Engaging and Valuable Content:

Create and share diverse content that resonates with your audience and adds value to their social media experience.

Mix content types such as product photos, videos, blog posts, user-generated content, behind-the-scenes glimpses, and industry news to keep your feed dynamic and engaging.

Use storytelling techniques, humor, and emotion to captivate your audience and encourage interaction and sharing.

Optimize Content for Each Platform:

Tailor your content to the unique characteristics and audience preferences of each social media platform.

Format content appropriately for each platform's specifications, such as image dimensions, video length, and caption length, to ensure optimal visibility and engagement.

Experiment with different content formats, hashtags, and posting times to maximize reach and engagement on each platform.

Build and Engage Your Audience:

Cultivate a loyal and engaged following by actively interacting with your audience through likes, comments, shares, and direct messages.

Respond promptly to customer inquiries, feedback, and comments to demonstrate responsiveness and build trust with your audience.

Encourage user-generated content and participation by running contests, giveaways, and interactive campaigns that

72

encourage audience participation and engagement.

Utilize Social Media Advertising:

Leverage social media advertising platforms such as Facebook Ads, Instagram Ads, Twitter Ads, LinkedIn Ads, and Pinterest Ads to amplify your reach and target specific audience segments.

Set clear campaign objectives, audience targeting parameters, and budget allocations to optimize ad performance and maximize return on investment (ROI).

Test different ad formats, creative elements, and targeting options to identify the most effective strategies for driving traffic and increasing sales.

Promote Your Shopify Store and Products:

Feature your Shopify store and product offerings prominently in your social media content and advertising campaigns.

Use compelling visuals, persuasive messaging, and clear calls-to-action (CTAs) to drive traffic to your Shopify store and encourage conversions.

Create shoppable posts and product tags to streamline the purchasing process and make it easier for users to discover and buy your products directly from social media platforms.

Track and Analyze Performance Metrics:

Monitor key performance indicators (KPIs) such as reach, engagement, click-through rates (CTRs), conversion rates, and sales revenue generated from social media marketing efforts.

Use social media analytics tools and built-in platform insights to track campaign performance, identify trends, and gain actionable insights into audience behavior and preferences.

Adjust your social media marketing strategies and tactics based on data-driven insights to optimize performance and achieve your business objectives over time.

Identifying the Most Effective Social Media Platforms for Your Audience

When it comes to leveraging social media for driving traffic and increasing sales on your Shopify store, it's essential to identify the most effective platforms where your target audience spends their time. Not all social media platforms are created equal, and understanding the demographics, preferences, and behavior of your audience can help you focus your efforts on the platforms that offer the greatest potential for engagement and conversion. Here's how to identify the most effective social media platforms for your audience:

Know Your Target Audience:

Start by developing a clear understanding of your target audience's demographics, interests, behaviors, and preferences.

Consider factors such as age, gender, location, income level, education, lifestyle, and psychographic characteristics when defining your target audience personas.

Conduct Audience Research:

Use data analytics tools, customer surveys, and market research to gather insights into your audience's social media usage habits, platform preferences, and content consumption behaviors.

Analyze existing customer data, website analytics, and social media engagement metrics to identify which platforms drive the most traffic, engagement, and conversions for your Shopify store.

Consider Platform Demographics:

Research the demographics and user profiles of different social media platforms to determine which ones align most closely with your target audience.

Consider factors such as age distribution, gender breakdown, income level, education level, and interests to assess the platform's relevance to your audience.

Evaluate Platform Features and Capabilities:

Evaluate the features, functionalities, and advertising options available on each social media platform to determine their

76

suitability for achieving your marketing objectives.

Consider factors such as content formats, targeting options, ad formats, retargeting capabilities, and performance tracking tools when assessing the effectiveness of each platform.

Understand User Intent and Behavior:

Consider the user intent and behavior associated with each social media platform to align your content and messaging with the platform's purpose and audience expectations.

Understand how users engage with content on each platform, including browsing habits, content consumption patterns, sharing behaviors, and purchase intent.

Assess Competitive Landscape:

Analyze the social media presence and performance of your competitors and industry peers to identify which platforms they are active on and where they are seeing success.

Look for opportunities to differentiate your brand and target audience segments on platforms that may be less saturated or overlooked by competitors.

Test and Iterate:

Experiment with different social media platforms and content strategies to gauge audience response and effectiveness.

Monitor key performance indicators (KPIs) such as engagement rates, click-through rates (CTRs), conversion rates, and return on investment (ROI) to evaluate the impact of your social media efforts.

Continuously test and iterate your social media marketing strategies based on data-driven insights and feedback to optimize performance and achieve your business objectives.

Creating Engaging Content for Social Media Channels

In the realm of ecommerce, creating engaging content for social media channels is pivotal for driving traffic, increasing brand visibility, and ultimately boosting sales on your Shopify store. Crafting content that resonates with your audience, sparks conversations, and encourages interactions is key to building a vibrant and active social media presence. Here are some strategies for creating engaging content for your social media channels:

Understand Your Audience:

Develop a deep understanding of your target audience's demographics, interests, preferences, and pain points.

Conduct audience research, analyze customer data, and gather insights from social media analytics to inform your content strategy.

Create Compelling Visuals:

Visual content is highly engaging and often performs better than text-only posts on social media.

Use high-quality images, videos, GIFs, infographics, and animations to capture attention and convey your brand message effectively.

Experiment with different visual formats and styles to keep your content fresh and visually appealing.

Tell Stories and Share Experiences:

Storytelling is a powerful way to connect with your audience on an emotional level and build brand affinity.

Share behind-the-scenes stories, customer testimonials, success stories, and user-generated content that highlights real experiences and humanizes your brand.

Use storytelling techniques such as narrative arcs, character development, and conflict resolution to create compelling narratives that resonate with your audience.

Educate and Inform Your Audience:

Provide valuable and educational content that addresses your audience's needs, interests, and pain points.

Share how-to guides, tutorials, tips, best practices, industry insights, and actionable advice that help your audience solve problems and achieve their goals.

Position your brand as a trusted authority in your niche by sharing informative and relevant content that adds value to your audience's lives.

Entertain and Delight Your Audience:

Social media users often seek entertainment and inspiration from the content they consume.

Incorporate humor, wit, creativity, and entertainment value into your posts to captivate your audience's attention and foster positive associations with your brand.

Share entertaining content such as memes, jokes, funny anecdotes, and lighthearted stories that resonate with your audience's sense of humor and personality.

Encourage User Engagement and Participation:

Foster a sense of community and belonging by encouraging user engagement and participation on your social media channels.

Pose questions, polls, quizzes, and challenges that prompt audience interaction and invite them to share their thoughts, opinions, and experiences.

81

Respond promptly to comments, messages, and mentions to show appreciation for audience engagement and cultivate meaningful connections with your followers.

Promote User-Generated Content (UGC):

Showcase user-generated content such as customer reviews, testimonials, photos, videos, and stories that feature your products or brand.

Encourage customers to share their experiences with your products and tag your brand on social media platforms.

Repost and share UGC on your social media channels to amplify its reach, build social proof, and foster a sense of community around your brand.

Offer Exclusive Deals and Promotions:

Create excitement and urgency by offering exclusive deals, promotions, discounts, and giveaways to your social media followers.

Use limited-time offers, flash sales, and social media-only discounts to incentivize

82

engagement and drive traffic to your Shopify store.

Use compelling visuals, persuasive messaging, and clear calls-to-action to encourage followers to take advantage of your offers.

Be Authentic and Transparent:

Authenticity and transparency are key to building trust and credibility with your audience on social media.

Be genuine, honest, and transparent in your communication and interactions with followers.

Share authentic stories, values, and experiences that reflect the personality and ethos of your brand.

Monitor Performance and Iterate:

Track key performance indicators (KPIs) such as engagement rates, reach, impressions, click-through rates (CTRs), and conversion metrics.

Use social media analytics tools and platform insights to analyze content performance, identify trends, and glean actionable insights.

Continuously test and iterate your content strategy based on data-driven insights and feedback to optimize engagement and drive results.

Leveraging Influencer Partnerships and Collaborations

In today's digital landscape, influencer marketing has emerged as a powerful strategy for driving traffic, increasing brand awareness, and boosting sales on Shopify stores. By partnering with influencers who have a dedicated and engaged following, you can tap into their credibility, authenticity, and reach to connect with your target audience and drive meaningful results for your ecommerce business. Here's how to leverage influencer partnerships and collaborations effectively:

Identify Relevant Influencers:

Conduct thorough research to identify influencers whose content, values, and audience align closely with your brand and target market.

Consider factors such as audience demographics, engagement rates, content quality, niche relevance, and brand affinity when evaluating potential influencers for partnership.

Build Authentic Relationships:

Approach influencer partnerships with a focus on building genuine and mutually beneficial relationships.

Take the time to engage with influencers authentically by liking, commenting, and sharing their content, and expressing genuine interest in their work and expertise.

Establish open and transparent communication channels to discuss collaboration opportunities and align expectations from the outset.

Define Clear Objectives and Goals:

Clearly define your objectives and goals for influencer partnerships, whether it's to increase brand awareness, drive website traffic, generate leads, or boost sales.

Align your goals with key performance indicators (KPIs) such as reach, engagement, click-through rates (CTRs), conversion rates, and return on investment (ROI) to measure the success of your influencer campaigns.

Craft Compelling Collaboration Briefs:

Develop collaboration briefs that outline the scope, deliverables, timeline, and compensation structure for influencer partnerships.

Clearly communicate your brand messaging, campaign objectives, creative direction, and any specific guidelines or requirements for content creation.

Provide influencers with the creative freedom and flexibility to tailor their content to their unique style and audience preferences while staying true to your brand identity and values.

Create Valuable and Authentic Content:

Encourage influencers to create authentic, relatable, and value-driven content that resonates with their audience and aligns with your brand's messaging and values.

Collaborate with influencers to develop engaging and creative content formats such as sponsored posts, product reviews, unboxing videos, tutorials, behind-the-scenes footage, and influencer takeovers.

Ensure that sponsored content is clearly disclosed as paid partnerships in compliance with applicable regulations and industry guidelines.

Amplify Reach and Engagement:

Leverage the influencer's reach and audience engagement to amplify the visibility and impact of your brand messaging and campaigns.

Promote influencer-created content across your own social media channels, website, email newsletters, and other marketing channels to extend its reach and engagement.

Encourage influencers to cross-promote sponsored content on their own social media platforms and engage with their audience to drive traffic and conversions.

Track and Measure Performance:

Implement tracking mechanisms and analytics tools to monitor the performance and effectiveness of influencer campaigns in real-time.

Track key performance metrics such as impressions, reach, engagement, click-through rates (CTRs), conversion rates, and revenue generated from influencer-driven traffic.

Use data-driven insights and performance metrics to evaluate the impact of influencer partnerships, identify areas for optimization, and refine your influencer marketing strategy over time.

Nurture Long-Term Relationships:

Foster ongoing relationships with influencers based on trust, respect, and mutual collaboration.

Recognize and appreciate the contributions of influencers by providing timely feedback, acknowledging their efforts, and offering opportunities for continued collaboration and partnership.

Maintain open lines of communication and seek feedback from influencers to continuously improve your influencer marketing initiatives and deliver greater value to both parties.

By leveraging influencer partnerships and collaborations effectively, you can harness the influence and credibility of trusted voices to amplify your brand message, drive targeted traffic, and increase sales on your Shopify store. By cultivating authentic and meaningful relationships with influencers, delivering valuable and engaging content to their audiences, and measuring the impact of influencer campaigns, you can unlock the full potential of influencer marketing as a strategic driver of growth and success for your ecommerce business.

Using Paid Advertising on Social Media Platforms

Paid advertising on social media platforms is a powerful strategy for generating traffic, increasing brand visibility, and driving sales on your Shopify store. With advanced targeting options, robust analytics, and flexible budgeting, social media advertising allows you to reach your target audience with precision and efficiency. Here's how to effectively use paid advertising on social media platforms to connect with your audience and achieve your business goals:

Set Clear Objectives and Goals:

Define specific objectives and goals for your social media advertising campaigns, such as increasing website traffic, generating leads, driving conversions, or boosting brand awareness.

Align your advertising goals with your overall business objectives and key performance indicators (KPIs) to measure the success and effectiveness of your campaigns.

Choose the Right Social Media Platforms:

Select the social media platforms that align best with your target audience, industry, and advertising objectives.

Consider factors such as audience demographics, interests, behavior, and platform features when determining where to allocate your advertising budget.

Identify Your Target Audience:

Utilize advanced targeting options and audience segmentation tools provided by social media advertising platforms to reach your ideal customers.

Define your target audience based on demographics, interests, behaviors, geographic location, purchase history, and other relevant criteria to ensure that your ads are shown to the most relevant and receptive audience segments.

Create Compelling Ad Creative:

Develop visually appealing and compelling ad creative that captures attention, communicates your value proposition, and drives action.

Use high-quality images, videos, graphics, and ad copy that resonate with your target audience and align with your brand identity and messaging.

Experiment with different ad formats, such as carousel ads, video ads, slideshow ads, and interactive ads, to keep your campaigns fresh and engaging.

91

Craft Persuasive Ad Copy:

Write clear, concise, and persuasive ad copy that highlights the benefits of your products or services and encourages users to take action.

Use compelling headlines, descriptive language, and strong calls-to-action (CTAs) to prompt users to click on your ads, visit your Shopify store, and make a purchase.

Test different messaging variations and CTAs to identify which resonate most effectively with your target audience and drive the desired outcomes.

Set Budgets and Bidding Strategies:

Determine your advertising budgets and bidding strategies based on your campaign objectives, target audience, and desired outcomes.

Allocate your budget strategically across different campaigns, ad sets, and audience segments to maximize reach, engagement, and conversion opportunities.

Monitor your ad spend, cost per click (CPC), cost per acquisition (CPA), and return on ad spend (ROAS) closely to ensure that your campaigns are delivering optimal results within your budget constraints.

Optimize Targeting and Ad Performance:

Continuously refine and optimize your targeting parameters, ad creative, and messaging based on performance data and audience insights.

A/B test different audience segments, ad placements, ad formats, creative elements, and messaging variations to identify winning combinations and maximize campaign effectiveness.

Use split testing, ad rotation, and ad scheduling features to experiment with different variables and optimize your campaigns for maximum impact and efficiency.

Track and Measure Results:

Use analytics and reporting tools provided by social media advertising platforms to track and measure the performance of your campaigns in real-time.

Monitor key performance indicators (KPIs) such as impressions, clicks, click-through rates (CTRs), conversions, conversion rates, and return on investment (ROI) to evaluate the effectiveness and ROI of your advertising efforts.

Use performance data and insights to identify trends, patterns, and opportunities for optimization, and make data-driven decisions to improve campaign performance and achieve your advertising goals.

Stay Compliant and Adhere to Best Practices:

Familiarize yourself with the advertising policies, guidelines, and best practices of each social media platform to ensure compliance and maximize the effectiveness of your campaigns.

Adhere to relevant regulations and guidelines related to data privacy, consumer protection, and advertising disclosures to maintain transparency and trust with your audience.

Stay informed about changes and updates to advertising algorithms, targeting options, and ad formats on social media platforms, and adjust your strategies accordingly to stay ahead of the curve.

By leveraging paid advertising on social media platforms effectively, you can reach your target audience with precision, drive targeted traffic to your Shopify store, and increase sales and conversions. By setting clear objectives, defining your target audience, creating compelling ad creative, optimizing campaign performance, and measuring results, you can maximize the impact and ROI of your social media advertising efforts and achieve sustainable growth and success for your ecommerce business.

CHAPTER 5

SEARCH ENGINE MARKETING (SEM) AND PAY-PER-CLICK (PPC) ADVERTISING

Search Engine Marketing (SEM) and Pay-Per-Click (PPC) advertising are essential components of any comprehensive digital marketing strategy aimed at generating traffic and increasing sales on your Shopify store. SEM and PPC campaigns allow you to place targeted ads on search engine results pages (SERPs) and across various digital platforms, reaching potential customers actively searching for products or services like yours. Here's how to leverage SEM and PPC advertising effectively:

Keyword Research and Selection

Conduct thorough keyword research to identify relevant search terms and phrases that your target audience is using to find products or services similar to yours.

Use keyword research tools, such as Google Keyword Planner, SEMrush, and Ahrefs, to discover high-volume keywords, long-tail keywords, and related terms with strong commercial intent.

Prioritize keywords that are relevant to your products, have high search volume, and demonstrate strong buying intent to maximize the effectiveness of your PPC campaigns.

Create Compelling Ad Copy:

Develop engaging and persuasive ad copy that resonates with your target audience and encourages clicks and conversions.

Write clear, concise, and compelling headlines and descriptions that highlight the unique selling points and benefits of your products or services.

Use action-oriented language, compelling offers, and strong calls-to-action (CTAs) to prompt users to take the desired action, such as clicking on your ad or making a purchase.

Optimize Landing Pages:

Design and optimize dedicated landing pages that align closely with the messaging and offer presented in your PPC ads.

Ensure that landing pages load quickly, are mobile-friendly, and provide a seamless user experience across devices.

Include relevant and persuasive content, prominent CTAs, and clear pathways to conversion to maximize the effectiveness of your PPC campaigns and improve conversion rates.

Set Up Conversion Tracking:

Implement conversion tracking mechanisms, such as Google Analytics conversion tracking or Facebook Pixel, to measure the performance and effectiveness of your PPC campaigns.

Track key performance indicators (KPIs) such as click-through rates (CTRs), conversion rates, cost per acquisition (CPA), return on ad spend (ROAS), and overall campaign ROI to evaluate the success of your campaigns and identify areas for improvement.

Segment and Target Your Audience:

Utilize audience segmentation and targeting options to reach specific audience segments with tailored messaging and offers.

Leverage demographic targeting, geographic targeting, device targeting, and audience interests to refine your targeting parameters and ensure that your ads are shown to the most relevant and receptive audience segments.

Use retargeting and remarketing strategies to re-engage users who have previously visited your website or interacted with your brand but have not yet converted into customers.

Monitor and Optimize Campaign Performance:

Monitor the performance of your SEM and PPC campaigns closely and make data-driven decisions to optimize performance and maximize ROI.

Regularly review key metrics and performance indicators to identify trends, patterns, and opportunities for improvement.

Adjust your bidding strategies, ad placements, targeting parameters, and ad creatives based on performance data and insights to improve campaign effectiveness and efficiency over time.

Test and Iterate:

Implement A/B testing and experimentation techniques to test different ad creatives, messaging variations, landing page designs, and targeting strategies.

Test one variable at a time, such as headline copy, ad imagery, or targeting parameters, to isolate the impact of each change and identify winning combinations.

Use testing and iteration to continuously refine and optimize your SEM and PPC campaigns for maximum performance and results.

Stay Updated and Adapt to Changes:

Stay informed about changes, updates, and trends in the SEM and PPC advertising landscape, including algorithm updates, platform features, and industry best practices.

Adapt your strategies and tactics accordingly to stay ahead of the competition and capitalize on emerging opportunities for growth and optimization.

Participate in industry forums, webinars, and conferences, and leverage resources such as blogs, podcasts, and online courses to stay informed and continuously improve your SEM and PPC advertising skills.

By implementing these strategies effectively, you can leverage SEM and PPC advertising to drive targeted traffic, increase brand visibility, and drive sales and conversions on your Shopify store. By conducting thorough keyword research, creating compelling ad copy, optimizing landing pages, tracking conversions, targeting specific audience segments, monitoring campaign performance, testing and iterating, and staying updated on industry trends, you can maximize the impact and ROI of your SEM and PPC advertising efforts and achieve sustainable growth and success for your ecommerce business.

101

Understanding Google Ads and Bing Ads

Google Ads and Bing Ads are two of the most prominent platforms for running pay-per-click (PPC) advertising campaigns, offering powerful tools and extensive reach to help Shopify store owners generate traffic and increase sales. Understanding how to effectively utilize these advertising platforms is essential for maximizing your ecommerce success. Here's a comprehensive overview of Google Ads and Bing Ads:

Google Ads:

Google Ads, formerly known as Google AdWords, is Google's advertising platform that allows advertisers to display ads on Google's search engine results pages (SERPs), as well as on the Google Display Network (GDN) and YouTube.

With Google Ads, advertisers bid on keywords relevant to their products or services, and their ads appear alongside organic search results when users enter those keywords into Google's search engine.

Google Ads offers a variety of ad formats, including text ads, display ads, video ads, shopping ads, and app ads, allowing advertisers to reach their target audience through different channels and formats.

Google Ads provides robust targeting options, including keyword targeting, location targeting, demographic targeting, device targeting, and audience targeting, enabling advertisers to reach specific audience segments with tailored messaging and offers.

Google Ads offers advanced bidding options, including manual bidding, automated bidding strategies (such as target CPA, target ROAS, and maximize clicks), and smart bidding algorithms that optimize bids in real-time based on performance data and objectives.

Google Ads provides detailed analytics and reporting tools that allow advertisers to track and measure the performance of their campaigns, including metrics such as impressions, clicks, click-through rates (CTRs), conversions, conversion rates, cost per acquisition (CPA), and return on ad spend (ROAS).

103

Bing Ads:

Bing Ads is Microsoft's advertising platform that allows advertisers to display ads on the Bing search engine, as well as on Yahoo, AOL, and other partner sites within the Bing Network.

Bing Ads operates similarly to Google Ads, allowing advertisers to bid on keywords and display ads alongside search results when users enter relevant search queries into the Bing search engine.

Bing Ads offers a range of ad formats, including text ads, shopping ads, and image ads, enabling advertisers to engage with their target audience through various channels and formats.

Bing Ads provides targeting options such as keyword targeting, location targeting, demographic targeting, device targeting, and audience targeting, allowing advertisers to reach specific audience segments with precision.

Bing Ads offers flexible bidding options, including manual bidding and automated bidding strategies (such as enhanced CPC and target CPA), enabling advertisers to optimize bids and maximize performance based on their campaign objectives and budget constraints.

Bing Ads provides comprehensive reporting and analytics tools that allow advertisers to track and analyze the performance of their campaigns, monitor key metrics, and gain actionable insights to inform decision-making and optimization efforts.

Key Similarities Between Google Ads and Bing Ads:

Both Google Ads and Bing Ads operate on a pay-per-click (PPC) pricing model, where advertisers only pay when users click on their ads.

Both platforms offer robust targeting options, ad formats, and bidding strategies to help advertisers reach their target audience and achieve their advertising goals.

Both Google Ads and Bing Ads provide analytics and reporting tools that allow advertisers to track and measure the performance of their campaigns, optimize bidding strategies, and maximize return on investment (ROI).

105

Key Differences Between Google Ads and Bing Ads:

Audience Reach: Google Ads has a significantly larger audience reach compared to Bing Ads, as Google dominates the search engine market with a higher market share.

Cost Per Click (CPC): In general, CPC tends to be lower on Bing Ads compared to Google Ads, making it a more cost-effective option for advertisers with smaller budgets.

Audience Demographics: Bing Ads typically attract an older and more affluent demographic compared to Google Ads, making it a valuable platform for advertisers targeting specific demographic segments.

User Intent: Users on Bing may exhibit different search behaviors and intent compared to Google users, which can influence the performance and effectiveness of advertising campaigns on each platform.

Keyword Research and Targeting

Keyword research and targeting are fundamental aspects of any successful digital marketing strategy, especially for Shopify store owners aiming to generate traffic and increase sales. By understanding the search terms and phrases your target audience uses, you can optimize your website content, PPC campaigns, and SEO efforts to attract qualified traffic and drive conversions. Here's how to effectively conduct keyword research and targeting for your Shopify store:

Understand Your Audience:

Start by gaining a deep understanding of your target audience, including their demographics, interests, preferences, and search behavior.

Identify the pain points, needs, and motivations that drive your audience's search queries and purchase decisions.

Brainstorm Seed Keywords:

Begin your keyword research process by brainstorming a list of seed keywords

107

relevant to your Shopify store, products, and industry.

Think about the primary categories, products, features, benefits, and solutions that your target audience may be searching for online.

Utilize Keyword Research Tools:

Use keyword research tools such as Google Keyword Planner, SEMrush, Ahrefs, Moz Keyword Explorer, and Ubersuggest to discover relevant keywords and search volume data.

Enter your seed keywords into these tools to generate a list of related keywords, long-tail keywords, and search queries that your audience may be using.

Focus on Long-Tail Keywords:

Long-tail keywords are specific, niche-focused search queries that typically have lower search volume but higher intent and conversion potential.

Target long-tail keywords that are relevant to your products, address specific customer needs, and have less competition compared to broader, generic keywords.

Consider Commercial Intent:

Evaluate the commercial intent behind different keywords to prioritize those with strong buying intent and conversion potential.

Look for keywords that include transactional terms such as "buy," "shop," "order," "discount," or specific product names and models.

Assess Keyword Competition:

Analyze the competitiveness of keywords by assessing factors such as search volume, keyword difficulty, and competition level.

Focus on targeting keywords with a balance of search volume and competition that align with your budget and resources.

Optimize for User Intent:

Consider the user's intent behind their search queries and tailor your keyword targeting and content strategy accordingly.

Identify the different types of user intent, including informational, navigational, and transactional, and create content that satisfies each type of intent.

109

Implement On-Page Optimization:

Incorporate your target keywords strategically throughout your Shopify store, including in product titles, descriptions, meta tags, headings, and alt text for images.

Optimize your website content to provide valuable and relevant information that matches the user's search intent and addresses their needs effectively.

Monitor Performance and Iterate:

Regularly monitor the performance of your targeted keywords using analytics tools such as Google Analytics, Google Search Console, and Shopify's built-in analytics.

Track key metrics such as organic traffic, keyword rankings, click-through rates (CTRs), conversion rates, and revenue generated from keyword-targeted traffic.

Use performance data and insights to identify trends, opportunities, and areas for optimization, and adjust your keyword targeting and content strategy accordingly.

110

Creating Effective Ad Copy and Landing Pages

Creating compelling ad copy and landing pages is crucial for Shopify store owners looking to generate traffic and increase sales through online advertising campaigns. Effective ad copy grabs the attention of your target audience, communicates your value proposition, and compels users to take action, while well-designed landing pages provide a seamless and persuasive user experience that drives conversions. Here's how to create effective ad copy and landing pages for your Shopify store:

Understand Your Audience:

Gain a deep understanding of your target audience's demographics, interests, pain points, and motivations.

Identify the key benefits and unique selling points of your products or services that resonate with your target audience.

Craft Compelling Ad Headlines:

Start with attention-grabbing headlines that capture the user's attention and entice them to learn more.

111

Use action-oriented language, power words, and emotional triggers to evoke curiosity and interest in your ad.

Highlight Key Benefits and Features:

Clearly communicate the unique benefits and features of your products or services that set them apart from the competition.

Focus on addressing the specific needs, desires, and pain points of your target audience to demonstrate the value proposition of your offer.

Include Persuasive Call-to-Actions (CTAs):

Use strong and compelling CTAs that encourage users to take the desired action, such as "Shop Now," "Learn More," "Get Started," or "Claim Your Discount."

Create a sense of urgency or scarcity by incorporating time-limited offers, limited stock availability, or exclusive deals into your CTAs.

Maintain Consistency and Relevance:

Ensure that your ad copy is consistent with the messaging and offer presented on your landing page.

Align your ad copy with the user's search intent and ensure that it delivers on the promises made in the ad.

Optimize for Keywords and Ad Relevance:

Incorporate relevant keywords into your ad copy to improve ad relevance and quality score.

Use dynamic keyword insertion (DKI) to customize your ad copy based on the user's search query and increase ad relevance.

Design Clear and Compelling Landing Pages:

Create landing pages that are visually appealing, user-friendly, and optimized for conversions.

Use clean and uncluttered design elements, intuitive navigation, and prominent CTAs to guide users through the conversion funnel.

113

Deliver Value and Address User Intent:

Provide valuable and relevant information that addresses the user's search intent and fulfills their needs and expectations.

Clearly communicate the benefits of your offer and how it solves the user's problem or meets their needs.

Optimize for Mobile Responsiveness:

Ensure that your landing pages are optimized for mobile devices and provide a seamless user experience across all screen sizes and devices.

Use responsive design principles, mobile-friendly layouts, and fast-loading content to enhance usability and reduce bounce rates.

Test and Iterate for Optimization:

Conduct A/B testing and multivariate testing to experiment with different ad copy variations, headlines, CTAs, and landing page designs.

Monitor key metrics such as click-through rates (CTRs), conversion rates, bounce rates, and time-on-page to identify winning combinations and optimize performance over time.

Implement Conversion Tracking and Analytics:

Set up conversion tracking and analytics tools to measure the performance and effectiveness of your ad campaigns and landing pages.

Track key metrics and KPIs to assess the ROI of your advertising efforts and identify areas for improvement and optimization.

Monitoring and Optimizing Ad Campaigns for Maximum ROI

Monitoring and optimizing ad campaigns is crucial for Shopify store owners aiming to generate traffic and increase sales effectively while maximizing return on investment (ROI). By continuously analyzing campaign performance, making data-driven decisions, and refining strategies, merchants can ensure that their advertising efforts yield the best possible results. Here's how to monitor and optimize ad campaigns for maximum ROI:

115

Establish Clear Objectives:

Define specific goals and objectives for your ad campaigns, such as increasing website traffic, generating leads, driving conversions, or boosting sales.

Ensure that your objectives are measurable, achievable, and aligned with your overall business goals and KPIs.

Track Key Performance Metrics:

Identify the key performance indicators (KPIs) that matter most to your campaign objectives, such as click-through rates (CTRs), conversion rates, cost per acquisition (CPA), return on ad spend (ROAS), and overall campaign ROI.

Implement tracking mechanisms and analytics tools to monitor and measure the performance of your ad campaigns in real-time.

Monitor Campaign Performance Regularly:

Regularly review and analyze campaign performance data to identify trends, patterns, and areas for improvement.

Monitor key metrics and KPIs to assess the effectiveness and efficiency of your ad

116

campaigns and identify any anomalies or issues that may arise.

Segment and Analyze Data:

Segment your campaign data by different variables such as demographics, geography, device type, ad placement, and audience segments.

Analyze performance data at a granular level to gain insights into which audience segments, ad creatives, and targeting parameters are driving the best results.

Identify High-Performing Tactics:

Identify the ad creatives, messaging variations, targeting strategies, and bidding techniques that are driving the highest ROI and conversion rates.

Double down on tactics and strategies that are delivering positive results and consider reallocating budget and resources accordingly.

Optimize Ad Creative and Messaging:

Continuously test and iterate on your ad creative and messaging to identify which

117

variations resonate most effectively with your target audience.

Experiment with different headlines, ad copy, images, videos, and calls-to-action (CTAs) to optimize engagement, click-through rates, and conversion rates.

Refine Targeting and Audience Segmentation:

Refine your targeting parameters and audience segmentation based on performance data and audience insights.

Adjust targeting options such as demographics, interests, behaviors, and geographic locations to reach the most relevant and receptive audience segments.

Adjust Bidding Strategies:

Adjust your bidding strategies and budget allocations based on campaign performance and desired outcomes.

Consider using automated bidding strategies, such as target CPA (cost per acquisition) or target ROAS (return on ad spend), to optimize bids and maximize performance while achieving your desired cost-per-conversion goals.

118

Implement Ad Scheduling and Frequency Capping:

Use ad scheduling to control when your ads are displayed to maximize visibility during peak times and minimize wasted spend during off-peak hours.

Implement frequency capping to limit the number of times your ads are shown to the same user within a specific time period, preventing ad fatigue and improving ad relevance.

Stay Abreast of Industry Trends and Best Practices:

Stay informed about changes, updates, and trends in the digital advertising landscape, including platform updates, algorithm changes, and emerging ad formats.

Participate in industry forums, webinars, and conferences, and leverage resources such as blogs, podcasts, and case studies to stay updated on the latest best practices and optimization techniques.

Iterate and Test Continuously:

Continuously iterate and test different variables, strategies, and tactics to optimize campaign performance and achieve maximum ROI.

Implement A/B testing and multivariate testing to experiment with different ad elements and parameters and identify winning combinations.

Document Insights and Learnings:

Document insights, learnings, and optimization strategies from your ad campaigns to inform future campaigns and initiatives.

Keep a record of successful tactics, performance trends, and lessons learned to build institutional knowledge and continuously improve your advertising efforts over time.

CHAPTER 6

UTILIZING ANALYTICS AND DATA-DRIVEN INSIGHTS

Analytics and data-driven insights are invaluable tools for Shopify store owners seeking to generate traffic and increase sales effectively. By harnessing the power of data, merchants can gain valuable insights into customer behavior, campaign performance, and website effectiveness, allowing them to make informed decisions and optimize their strategies for maximum results. Here's how to effectively utilize analytics and data-driven insights:

Implement Robust Analytics Tools

Set up comprehensive analytics tools such as Google Analytics, Shopify Analytics, and other third-party tracking platforms to monitor website traffic, user behavior, and conversion metrics.

Configure tracking codes, tags, and event triggers to capture relevant data points and insights across different stages of the customer journey.

Define Key Performance Indicators (KPIs):

Define clear and actionable key performance indicators (KPIs) aligned with your business objectives, such as website traffic, conversion rates, average order value (AOV), customer acquisition cost (CAC), and customer lifetime value (CLV).

Prioritize KPIs that directly impact your bottom line and reflect the effectiveness of your marketing efforts and sales performance.

Segment and Analyze Customer Data:

Segment your customer data based on demographics, geographic location, purchasing behavior, order history, and other relevant criteria to gain insights into different audience segments and buyer personas.

Analyze customer data to identify trends, patterns, and preferences that can inform product offerings, marketing strategies, and personalized messaging.

122

Monitor Website Traffic and User Behavior:

Track website traffic sources, referral sources, landing pages, exit pages, and user navigation paths to understand how visitors interact with your Shopify store.

Analyze user behavior metrics such as bounce rates, session duration, page views, and conversion funnels to identify areas for optimization and improvement.

Evaluate Campaign Performance:

Monitor the performance of your marketing campaigns across different channels, including paid advertising, social media, email marketing, and content marketing.

Evaluate campaign metrics such as click-through rates (CTRs), conversion rates, return on ad spend (ROAS), cost per acquisition (CPA), and attribution models to assess the effectiveness and ROI of your campaigns.

Track Ecommerce Metrics:

Track ecommerce-specific metrics such as product sales, revenue, average order value (AOV), conversion rates, cart

123

abandonment rates, and customer retention rates to measure the financial performance of your Shopify store.

Identify high-performing products, best-selling categories, and seasonal trends to optimize inventory management and merchandising strategies.

Utilize A/B Testing and Experimentation:

Implement A/B testing and experimentation techniques to test different variations of website elements, marketing messages, ad creatives, and landing page designs.

Conduct controlled experiments to measure the impact of changes and optimizations on key metrics and performance indicators.

Generate Reports and Dashboards:

Create customized reports, dashboards, and data visualizations to summarize key metrics and insights and facilitate data-driven decision-making.

Share reports and insights with relevant stakeholders across your organization to

124

foster collaboration and alignment around common goals and objectives.

Identify Opportunities for Optimization:

Identify opportunities for optimization and improvement based on data-driven insights and performance trends.

Prioritize initiatives that have the potential to drive significant impact and align with your strategic priorities and business objectives.

Iterate and Improve Continuously:

Continuously iterate and improve your strategies, tactics, and processes based on ongoing analysis and feedback.

Embrace a culture of continuous improvement and experimentation, where data-driven insights drive decision-making and innovation.

Setting up Google Analytics and Shopify Analytics

Setting up Google Analytics and Shopify Analytics is essential for Shopify store owners who want to track website performance, user behavior, and

125

conversion metrics effectively. By integrating these analytics platforms, merchants can gain valuable insights into their website traffic, customer interactions, and sales data, enabling them to make data-driven decisions and optimize their strategies for generating traffic and increasing sales. Here's how to set up Google Analytics and Shopify Analytics for your Shopify store:

Setting Up Google Analytics

a. Create a Google Analytics Account:

Visit the Google Analytics website (analytics.google.com) and sign in with your Google account or create a new account if you don't have one.

Follow the prompts to create a new Google Analytics account and property for your Shopify store.

b. Generate Tracking ID:

Once your account and property are set up, you'll receive a unique tracking ID (UA-XXXXXXXX-X).

Copy the tracking ID as you'll need to paste it into your Shopify store settings.

126

c. Install Google Analytics Tracking Code:

In your Shopify admin dashboard, go to Online Store > Preferences.

Scroll down to the Google Analytics section and paste your tracking ID into the provided field.

Click "Save" to apply the changes.

d. Verify Installation:

To verify that Google Analytics is installed correctly, visit your Shopify store and navigate to a few pages.

In Google Analytics, go to the Real-Time reporting section and check if your activity is being tracked in real-time.

Setting Up Shopify Analytics:

a. Access Shopify Analytics:

In your Shopify admin dashboard, navigate to Analytics > Overview.

Shopify provides built-in analytics tools that offer valuable insights into your store's performance, sales trends, and customer behavior.

127

b. Explore Analytics Reports:

Explore the different analytics reports available in Shopify, including sales reports, traffic reports, customer reports, and behavior reports.

Gain insights into key metrics such as total sales, average order value, conversion rate, top-performing products, and customer demographics.

c. Customize Reports:

Customize the date range and filters for your analytics reports to focus on specific time periods, product categories, or customer segments.

Use the "Export" feature to download reports in various formats for further analysis and sharing with stakeholders.

d. Set Up Goals and Conversions:

Define specific goals and conversion events in Shopify, such as completed purchases, newsletter sign-ups, or account registrations.

Track goal completions and conversion rates to measure the effectiveness of your marketing campaigns and website optimization efforts.

e. Utilize Shopify Apps:

Explore third-party Shopify apps and integrations that extend the functionality of Shopify Analytics and provide additional insights and reporting capabilities.

Install apps that offer advanced analytics, customer segmentation, and predictive analytics to unlock deeper insights and drive informed decision-making.

Optimize Tracking and Configuration:

a. Enable Enhanced Ecommerce Tracking (Google Analytics):

Enable Enhanced Ecommerce Tracking in Google Analytics to track detailed ecommerce metrics such as product impressions, add-to-cart actions, and checkout behavior.

Configure Enhanced Ecommerce settings in your Google Analytics account and update your tracking code accordingly.

129

b. Review and Update Settings:

Regularly review and update your Google Analytics and Shopify Analytics settings to ensure accurate tracking and reporting.

Stay informed about new features, updates, and best practices for analytics configuration and implementation.

Analyzing Website Traffic, User Behavior, and Conversion Rates

Analyzing website traffic, user behavior, and conversion rates is essential for Shopify store owners who want to understand how visitors interact with their website, identify areas for improvement, and optimize their strategies for generating traffic and increasing sales effectively. By gaining insights into visitor demographics, browsing patterns, and conversion funnels, merchants can make informed decisions and drive sustainable growth for their ecommerce business. Here's how to analyze website traffic, user behavior, and conversion rates:

130

Traffic Sources Analysis:

Identify the sources of traffic to your Shopify store, including organic search, direct traffic, referral traffic, social media, email marketing, and paid advertising.

Analyze traffic sources to understand which channels drive the most visitors and which ones contribute to the highest conversion rates.

Determine the effectiveness of your marketing campaigns and optimize your budget allocation based on the performance of different traffic sources.

Demographic Insights:

Gain insights into the demographics of your website visitors, including age, gender, location, language, and device preferences.

Use demographic data to tailor your marketing messages, product offerings, and website experience to better resonate with your target audience.

User Behavior Analysis:

Analyze user behavior metrics such as bounce rate, session duration, pages per session, and behavior flow to understand how visitors navigate through your website.

131

Identify high-traffic pages, popular content, and common drop-off points to optimize your website structure, navigation menus, and content layout for improved user experience.

Conversion Funnel Analysis:

Map out the conversion funnel on your Shopify store, from initial visitor interaction to final purchase completion.

Analyze conversion rates at each stage of the funnel, including product views, add-to-cart actions, checkout initiation, and order completion.

Identify potential bottlenecks and friction points within the conversion funnel and implement optimizations to reduce barriers to conversion.

Product Performance Evaluation:

Evaluate the performance of your products based on metrics such as product views, add-to-cart rates, and conversion rates.

Identify top-selling products, best-performing categories, and underperforming items that may require additional promotion or optimization.

Use product performance data to optimize your product assortment, pricing strategies, and merchandising efforts.

Cart Abandonment Analysis:

Analyze cart abandonment rates and identify the reasons why users abandon their carts before completing the checkout process.

Implement cart abandonment recovery strategies such as email retargeting campaigns, exit-intent pop-ups, and incentive offers to encourage users to complete their purchase.

Attribution Modeling and Multi-Touch Analysis:

Implement attribution modeling to understand the contribution of different marketing channels and touchpoints to the conversion process.

Analyze multi-touch attribution data to assess the impact of cross-channel interactions and determine the most effective combination of marketing channels for driving conversions.

A/B Testing and Experimentation:

Conduct A/B tests and experimentation to test different variations of website elements, product pages, pricing strategies, and marketing messages.

Measure the impact of changes on key metrics such as conversion rates, revenue, and average order value, and iterate based on the results.

Continuous Monitoring and Optimization:

Continuously monitor website traffic, user behavior, and conversion rates using analytics tools such as Google Analytics, Shopify Analytics, and third-party tracking platforms.

Identify trends, patterns, and performance anomalies in real-time and take proactive measures to address issues and capitalize on opportunities.

Regularly review and optimize your website content, marketing campaigns, and conversion funnel based on data-driven insights and best practices.

134

Using Data to Make Informed Decisions and Adjustments to Marketing Strategies

In the realm of Shopify stores, harnessing the power of data is paramount for making informed decisions and refining marketing strategies to generate traffic and increase sales effectively. By leveraging data-driven insights, Shopify store owners can optimize their marketing efforts, enhance customer engagement, and drive sustainable growth for their ecommerce business. Here's how to use data to make informed decisions and adjustments to marketing strategies:

Collect Comprehensive Data

Implement robust analytics tools such as Google Analytics, Shopify Analytics, and third-party tracking platforms to collect comprehensive data on website traffic, user behavior, and conversion metrics.

Ensure that your data collection methods are configured correctly and capture relevant metrics across different stages of the customer journey.

135

Define Key Performance Indicators (KPIs):

Define clear and actionable key performance indicators (KPIs) aligned with your business objectives, such as website traffic, conversion rates, customer acquisition cost (CAC), return on ad spend (ROAS), and customer lifetime value (CLV).

Prioritize KPIs that directly impact your bottom line and reflect the effectiveness of your marketing strategies and sales performance.

Segment and Analyze Data:

Segment your data by different variables such as demographics, geographic location, device type, traffic source, and customer behavior to gain deeper insights into audience segments and buyer personas.

Analyze data trends, patterns, and correlations to identify opportunities for optimization and areas for improvement in your marketing strategies.

Monitor Campaign Performance:

Monitor the performance of your marketing campaigns across different channels, including paid advertising, social media, email marketing, content marketing, and affiliate marketing.

Evaluate campaign metrics such as click-through rates (CTRs), conversion rates, cost per acquisition (CPA), and return on investment (ROI) to assess the effectiveness and ROI of your marketing efforts.

Identify High-Impact Strategies:

Identify the marketing channels, tactics, and strategies that drive the highest ROI and contribute most effectively to your business objectives.

Allocate budget and resources to high-impact strategies and prioritize initiatives that have the potential to drive significant results and achieve your growth targets.

Optimize Conversion Funnels:

Analyze conversion funnels and identify potential bottlenecks, friction points, and

137

drop-off points that hinder the conversion process.

Implement optimization strategies such as streamlined checkout processes, personalized product recommendations, and targeted messaging to improve conversion rates and drive more sales.

Implement A/B Testing and Experimentation:

Conduct A/B tests and experimentation to test different variations of marketing campaigns, ad creatives, landing pages, and promotional offers.

Measure the impact of changes on key metrics such as engagement, conversion rates, and revenue, and iterate based on the results to optimize performance.

Personalize Customer Experiences:

Leverage data insights to personalize customer experiences and deliver targeted messaging, product recommendations, and promotional offers based on individual preferences, browsing history, and purchase behavior.

138

Use segmentation and dynamic content delivery to tailor marketing communications to specific audience segments and increase relevance and engagement.

Stay Agile and Responsive:

Stay agile and responsive to changes in market dynamics, consumer behavior, and industry trends by continuously monitoring data trends and adjusting marketing strategies accordingly.

Be prepared to pivot and adapt your marketing strategies in response to emerging opportunities and challenges in the competitive landscape.

Document Learnings and Best Practices:

Document insights, learnings, and best practices from your data analysis and experimentation to build institutional knowledge and inform future marketing initiatives.

Share insights and recommendations with relevant stakeholders across your organization to foster collaboration and alignment around common goals and objectives.

A/B Testing and Experimentation to Optimize Performance

A/B testing and experimentation are powerful strategies for Shopify store owners seeking to optimize performance, enhance user experience, and increase conversions effectively. By systematically testing different variations of website elements, marketing messages, and promotional offers, merchants can gain valuable insights into customer preferences, identify winning strategies, and refine their tactics to drive sustainable growth for their ecommerce business. Here's how to implement A/B testing and experimentation effectively:

Define Clear Objectives:

Start by defining clear objectives and key performance indicators (KPIs) for your A/B testing experiments, such as increasing conversion rates, improving click-through rates, or boosting average order value (AOV).

140

Align your testing objectives with your business goals and prioritize initiatives that have the potential to drive significant impact.

Identify Testing Opportunities:

Identify areas of your Shopify store and marketing campaigns that are ripe for optimization and experimentation, such as product pages, checkout processes, landing pages, CTAs, email subject lines, and ad creatives.

Prioritize testing opportunities based on their potential to improve user experience, increase engagement, and drive conversions.

Formulate Hypotheses:

Formulate hypotheses based on insights from data analysis, user feedback, and industry best practices.

Clearly define the changes or variations you plan to test and articulate the expected impact on user behavior and performance metrics.

Create Test Variations:

Develop multiple variations of the element or feature you intend to test, such as

141

different headline copy, button colors, imagery, layout designs, pricing structures, or promotional incentives.

Ensure that each variation is distinct and measurable, allowing for clear comparison and analysis of results.

Implement Testing Tools:

Utilize A/B testing tools and platforms such as Google Optimize, Optimizely, VWO (Visual Website Optimizer), or built-in Shopify apps to conduct experiments and track results.

Set up experiments with proper controls and randomization to ensure accurate and unbiased results.

Run Experiments:

Implement A/B tests with defined test groups and control groups to compare the performance of different variations.

Monitor experiments closely and track key metrics and KPIs to measure the impact of each variation on user behavior and conversion rates.

142

Analyze Results:

Analyze the results of your A/B tests using statistical significance testing and hypothesis testing methods to determine the validity of the findings.

Evaluate the performance of each variation based on key metrics such as conversion rates, revenue, engagement, bounce rates, and session duration.

Draw Insights and Learnings:

Draw insights and learnings from the results of your experiments, including which variations performed best, what factors influenced user behavior, and why certain changes led to improved performance.

Document findings and observations to inform future testing initiatives and optimization strategies.

Iterate and Iterate:

Based on insights gleaned from A/B testing, iterate on successful variations and refine strategies to further optimize performance.

Continuously iterate and refine your website elements, marketing messages,

143

and conversion funnels based on data-driven insights and experimentation.

Scale Successful Strategies:

Scale successful A/B testing strategies and best-performing variations across your Shopify store and marketing campaigns to drive consistent results and maximize impact.

Incorporate winning elements and tactics into your long-term optimization and growth strategy.

Stay Agile and Adaptive:

Embrace a culture of experimentation and continuous improvement, where A/B testing is an ongoing process rather than a one-time activity.

Stay agile and adaptive to changes in user behavior, market trends, and competitive landscape, and be prepared to adjust strategies based on evolving insights and feedback.

CHAPTER 7

BUILDING CUSTOMER RELATIONSHIPS AND RETENTION

In the competitive landscape of ecommerce, building strong customer relationships and fostering loyalty is crucial for Shopify store owners aiming to generate traffic, increase sales, and sustain long-term growth. By prioritizing customer satisfaction, engagement, and retention, merchants can cultivate a loyal customer base, drive repeat purchases, and maximize customer lifetime value. Here are strategies for building customer relationships and retention:

Personalized Customer Experience:

Personalize the shopping experience by tailoring product recommendations, marketing messages, and promotions based on individual preferences, browsing history, and purchase behavior.

Use customer data and segmentation techniques to create targeted campaigns and communications that resonate with specific audience segments.

Responsive Customer Support:

Provide responsive and attentive customer support across multiple channels, including live chat, email, phone support, and social media platforms.

Address customer inquiries, concerns, and feedback promptly, and strive to exceed expectations with proactive assistance and problem resolution.

Create Compelling Content:

Create engaging and informative content that adds value to the customer experience, such as product tutorials, buying guides, blog posts, and multimedia content.

Use storytelling and visual storytelling techniques to connect with customers on a deeper level and foster emotional engagement with your brand.

146

Implement Loyalty Programs:

Implement loyalty programs and rewards initiatives to incentivize repeat purchases and encourage customer loyalty.

Offer rewards points, discounts, exclusive offers, and VIP perks to reward loyal customers for their continued support and engagement.

Send Personalized Communications:

Send personalized communications and follow-ups to customers at key touchpoints along their journey, such as post-purchase thank you messages, order confirmations, and shipping updates.

Use email marketing automation tools to create targeted email campaigns that deliver relevant content and offers based on customer preferences and behaviors.

Collect and Act on Feedback:

Collect feedback from customers through surveys, reviews, and social media interactions to gain insights into their preferences, pain points, and satisfaction levels.

Act on customer feedback by making improvements to products, services, and processes based on their input and suggestions.

Offer Exceptional Shopping Experience:

Optimize the shopping experience by ensuring your website is user-friendly, intuitive, and optimized for mobile devices.

Streamline the checkout process, minimize friction points, and offer multiple payment options to make it easy for customers to complete their purchase.

Provide Value-Added Services:

Offer value-added services such as free shipping, easy returns, extended warranties, and installation support to enhance the perceived value of your products and increase customer satisfaction.

Go above and beyond to delight customers with unexpected surprises and gestures of appreciation.

Stay Engaged on Social Media:

Maintain an active presence on social media platforms and engage with

148

customers through meaningful interactions, conversations, and community building.

Share user-generated content, customer testimonials, and behind-the-scenes glimpses to humanize your brand and foster a sense of belonging among your audience.

Monitor Customer Metrics:

Monitor key customer metrics such as customer lifetime value (CLV), retention rate, churn rate, and Net Promoter Score (NPS) to track the health of your customer relationships and identify areas for improvement.

Use customer analytics and insights to segment your customer base and tailor retention strategies to different audience segments.

Celebrate Milestones and Special Occasions:

Celebrate customer milestones, birthdays, anniversaries, and special occasions with personalized messages, exclusive offers, and surprise gifts.

Show genuine appreciation for your customers' loyalty and support, and make them feel valued as part of your community.

Providing Exceptional Customer Service and Support

Exceptional customer service and support are fundamental components of success for Shopify store owners aiming to generate traffic, increase sales, and build long-term customer loyalty. By prioritizing customer satisfaction, responsiveness, and problem resolution, merchants can create positive experiences that foster trust, loyalty, and advocacy among their customer base. Here are strategies for providing exceptional customer service and support:

Multi-Channel Support:

Offer customer support across multiple channels, including live chat, email, phone support, social media platforms, and helpdesk systems.

Provide customers with flexibility and convenience by offering various communication channels to reach out for assistance.

150

Prompt Response Times:

Prioritize timely responses to customer inquiries, questions, and concerns to demonstrate responsiveness and attentiveness.

Set clear expectations for response times and strive to exceed those expectations whenever possible.

Empathetic Communication:

Approach customer interactions with empathy, patience, and understanding, regardless of the nature of the inquiry or issue.

Listen actively to customers' concerns, acknowledge their feelings, and validate their experiences to build trust and rapport.

Knowledgeable Support Team:

Equip your support team with comprehensive product knowledge, troubleshooting skills, and resources to address a wide range of customer inquiries and issues.

Provide ongoing training and professional development opportunities to empower support agents to deliver exceptional service.

151

Self-Service Resources:

Develop self-service resources such as FAQs, knowledge bases, tutorials, and troubleshooting guides to empower customers to find answers to common questions and resolve issues independently.

Make self-service resources easily accessible and searchable on your website to enhance the customer experience.

Proactive Communication:

Anticipate potential customer concerns or issues and proactively communicate relevant information, updates, and solutions to mitigate problems before they arise.

Keep customers informed about order status, shipping updates, product availability, and any potential disruptions to service.

Resolution-Focused Approach:

Prioritize problem resolution and aim to resolve customer issues and inquiries promptly and effectively.

Empower support agents to take ownership of customer problems, escalate issues as

152

needed, and follow up to ensure satisfactory resolution.

Feedback Collection and Action:

Solicit feedback from customers about their support experiences through surveys, ratings, and reviews.

Act on customer feedback by identifying recurring issues, areas for improvement, and opportunities to enhance the support experience.

Continuous Improvement:

Continuously evaluate and refine your customer service processes, policies, and workflows based on feedback, performance metrics, and industry best practices.

Foster a culture of continuous improvement and innovation within your support team to adapt to changing customer needs and expectations.

Measure Customer Satisfaction:

Monitor key performance indicators (KPIs) such as customer satisfaction scores (CSAT), Net Promoter Score (NPS), and customer retention rates to gauge the effectiveness of your customer service efforts.

153

Use customer feedback and satisfaction metrics to identify areas of strength and areas for improvement within your support operations.

Celebrate Successes and Recognize Excellence:

Recognize and celebrate exceptional customer service achievements and instances of going above and beyond to delight customers.

Acknowledge and reward support team members for their dedication, professionalism, and commitment to delivering exceptional customer experiences.

Implementing Loyalty Programs and Incentives

Loyalty programs and incentives play a crucial role in Shopify store owners' efforts to generate traffic, increase sales, and cultivate long-term customer loyalty. By rewarding customers for their repeat purchases, engagement, and advocacy, merchants can incentivize loyalty, drive customer retention, and maximize customer lifetime value. Here's how to implement effective loyalty programs and incentives:

Define Program Objectives:
Start by defining clear objectives for your loyalty program, such as increasing customer retention, boosting average order value (AOV), or encouraging customer referrals.

Align your program objectives with your overall business goals and target metrics for success.

Choose the Right Program Structure:
Select a loyalty program structure that best suits your business model and customer preferences, such as points-based programs, tiered loyalty tiers, cashback rewards, or VIP membership programs.

Design your program to be simple, transparent, and easy to understand for customers.

Reward Points for Purchases:
Reward customers with loyalty points or rewards for every purchase they make on your Shopify store.

155

Offer bonus points for specific actions such as signing up for an account, referring friends, writing product reviews, or engaging with your brand on social media.

Tiered Rewards System:

Implement a tiered rewards system where customers can unlock higher tiers and exclusive benefits as they accumulate more points or reach specific spending thresholds.

Create a sense of progression and exclusivity to incentivize customers to achieve higher tiers.

Personalized Rewards and Offers:

Personalize rewards and offers based on customer preferences, purchase history, and engagement level.

Offer targeted promotions, discounts, and incentives tailored to individual customer segments to enhance relevance and effectiveness.

Special Birthday and Anniversary Rewards:

Surprise and delight customers by offering special rewards, discounts, or gifts on their birthdays, anniversaries, or other significant milestones.

Show appreciation for their loyalty and celebrate their relationship with your brand.

Exclusive Access and Benefits:

Provide exclusive access to VIP perks, early access to sales, limited edition products, and special events for loyal customers.

Offer premium benefits such as free shipping, extended return windows, or dedicated customer support for VIP members.

Promote Program Visibility:

Prominently feature your loyalty program on your Shopify store website, including dedicated landing pages, banners, and pop-ups to encourage sign-ups and participation.

Clearly communicate the benefits, rewards, and earning opportunities associated with your program to incentivize customer engagement.

Track and Measure Program Performance:

Monitor key performance indicators (KPIs) such as enrollment rates, redemption rates, average order value (AOV), and customer retention rates to measure the effectiveness of your loyalty program.

Use data analytics and reporting tools to track customer engagement, identify trends, and optimize program incentives and rewards over time.

Continuously Evolve and Improve:

Solicit feedback from customers about their experiences with your loyalty program and use their input to refine and improve program offerings.

Stay informed about industry trends, best practices, and emerging technologies in loyalty marketing to adapt your program strategy and remain competitive.

Integrate with Marketing Campaigns:

Integrate your loyalty program with your marketing campaigns to drive customer engagement and participation.

Promote special offers, double points events, or bonus rewards to incentivize purchases and encourage program enrollment.

Personalizing the Shopping Experience through Targeted Marketing

Personalizing the shopping experience through targeted marketing is a powerful strategy for Shopify store owners looking to generate traffic, increase sales, and foster strong customer relationships. By leveraging customer data, segmentation techniques, and personalized messaging, merchants can create tailored experiences that resonate with individual preferences, behaviors, and needs. Here's how to personalize the shopping experience through targeted marketing:

Collect and Analyze Customer Data:

Utilize Shopify analytics tools and integrations to collect comprehensive customer data, including purchase history, browsing behavior, demographics, and preferences.

Analyze customer data to identify patterns, trends, and insights that inform targeted marketing strategies.

Segment Your Audience:

Segment your customer base into distinct audience segments based on shared characteristics, behaviors, and preferences.

Consider segmentation criteria such as demographics, geographic location, purchase frequency, order value, and product preferences.

Create Customer Personas:

Develop detailed customer personas representing different segments of your target audience.

Use personas to understand the unique needs, motivations, and pain points of each

160

segment and tailor marketing messages accordingly.

Implement Behavioral Targeting:

Leverage behavioral targeting techniques to deliver personalized marketing messages based on customer interactions and engagement with your Shopify store.

Serve relevant product recommendations, content, and promotions based on browsing history, abandoned carts, and past purchases.

Dynamic Product Recommendations:

Implement dynamic product recommendation widgets on your Shopify store to showcase personalized product suggestions based on individual browsing and purchase behavior.

Use algorithms to analyze customer preferences and suggest complementary or relevant products to enhance the shopping experience.

Personalized Email Marketing:

Craft personalized email campaigns that speak directly to the interests and preferences of each customer segment.

161

Segment email lists based on customer attributes and behaviors, and tailor messaging, offers, and content to match the interests of each segment.

Triggered Email Campaigns:

Set up triggered email campaigns to automatically send targeted messages in response to specific customer actions or events, such as abandoned carts, product views, or milestone anniversaries.

Use dynamic content and personalized subject lines to capture attention and drive engagement.

Optimize Website Personalization:

Implement website personalization techniques to deliver customized experiences to visitors based on their past interactions and preferences.

Display personalized product recommendations, content blocks, and promotional banners to engage visitors and encourage exploration.

Use Social Media Targeting:

Leverage social media advertising platforms to target specific audience segments with tailored ad campaigns.

Use demographic targeting, interest-based targeting, and retargeting techniques to reach customers with relevant offers and messages.

Test and Iterate:

Continuously test and iterate your targeted marketing strategies to optimize performance and effectiveness.

Monitor key metrics such as click-through rates, conversion rates, and revenue generated from personalized campaigns, and adjust your approach based on data-driven insights.

Respect Customer Privacy and Preferences:

Respect customer privacy and preferences by adhering to data protection regulations and allowing customers to control their communication preferences.

Provide options for customers to opt in or opt out of personalized marketing communications and respect their choices.

163

Encouraging Repeat Purchases and Referrals

Encouraging repeat purchases and referrals is essential for Shopify store owners seeking to generate traffic, increase sales, and foster long-term customer loyalty. By implementing strategies that incentivize customers to return and advocate for your brand, merchants can create a sustainable revenue stream and expand their customer base through word-of-mouth referrals. Here's how to encourage repeat purchases and referrals:

Offer Loyalty Rewards:

Implement a loyalty program that rewards customers for their repeat purchases and engagement with your Shopify store.

Offer points, discounts, or exclusive perks for every purchase made, encouraging customers to return and redeem their rewards.

Provide Excellent Customer Service:

Deliver exceptional customer service and support to create positive experiences that encourage customers to return.

Address inquiries and resolve issues promptly, exceeding customer expectations and building trust and loyalty.

Send Personalized Follow-Up Emails:

Send personalized follow-up emails to thank customers for their purchase and encourage them to return for future shopping.

Include personalized product recommendations, exclusive offers, or loyalty rewards to incentivize repeat purchases.

Offer Subscription Services:

Introduce subscription services for products that customers frequently purchase on a recurring basis.

Offer subscription discounts or perks to incentivize customers to sign up and automate their repeat purchases.

165

Implement Retargeting Campaigns:

Use retargeting campaigns to re-engage customers who have previously visited your Shopify store or abandoned their carts.

Serve personalized ads or promotional offers to encourage customers to return and complete their purchase.

Create a Seamless Shopping Experience:

Optimize your Shopify store for a seamless shopping experience across devices and channels.

Streamline the checkout process, offer multiple payment options, and provide transparent shipping and return policies to remove barriers to purchase.

Encourage Customer Reviews and Testimonials:

Encourage satisfied customers to leave reviews and testimonials about their shopping experience and products purchased.

Display customer reviews prominently on your Shopify store to build social proof and

166

trust, encouraging new customers to make a purchase.

Incentivize Referral Programs:

Implement a referral program that rewards customers for referring friends, family, or colleagues to your Shopify store.

Offer incentives such as discounts, credits, or exclusive offers for both the referrer and the new customer who makes a purchase.

Create Shareable Content and Social Proof:

Create shareable content such as blog posts, videos, or user-generated content that showcases your products and brand in a compelling light.

Encourage customers to share their purchases and experiences on social media platforms, amplifying your brand reach and driving referrals.

Host Exclusive Events and Sales:

Host exclusive events, sales, or product launches for loyal customers and subscribers.

Offer early access, special discounts, or VIP perks to reward their loyalty and encourage repeat purchases.

Track and Measure Performance:

Monitor key performance indicators (KPIs) such as customer retention rate, repeat purchase rate, and referral conversion rate to measure the effectiveness of your strategies.

Use data analytics to identify trends, insights, and opportunities for optimization, adjusting your approach based on performance metrics.

CHAPTER 8

SCALING YOUR SHOPIFY BUSINESS

Scaling your Shopify business is a multifaceted endeavor that involves expanding your operations, increasing your customer base, and maximizing your revenue potential. As you strive to grow your ecommerce venture, it's essential to adopt strategies that allow you to effectively manage growth while maintaining a focus on customer satisfaction and profitability. Here are key steps to scale your Shopify business:

Set Clear Goals and Objectives

Define specific, measurable goals and objectives that outline your vision for scaling your Shopify business.

Establish milestones and key performance indicators (KPIs) to track progress and evaluate the success of your scaling efforts.

Optimize Your Ecommerce Infrastructure:

Assess and optimize your Shopify store's infrastructure to accommodate increased traffic, transactions, and inventory management.

Ensure that your website is scalable, reliable, and capable of handling peak demand without sacrificing performance.

Streamline Business Processes:

Streamline and automate key business processes such as order fulfillment, inventory management, and customer support to improve efficiency and scalability.

Invest in tools and software solutions that streamline workflows and enable seamless integration with your Shopify platform.

Expand Product Offerings:

Diversify and expand your product offerings to appeal to a broader audience and capture new market segments.

Conduct market research to identify emerging trends, niche markets, and product categories with high demand potential.

Invest in Marketing and Advertising:

Allocate resources to marketing and advertising initiatives that drive traffic, increase brand visibility, and generate sales.

Implement targeted marketing campaigns across multiple channels, including social media, email marketing, search engine optimization (SEO), and pay-per-click (PPC) advertising.

Enhance Customer Experience:

Prioritize customer experience initiatives that enhance satisfaction, loyalty, and retention rates.

Offer personalized shopping experiences, exceptional customer service, and seamless checkout processes to create positive interactions at every touchpoint.

Build Strategic Partnerships:

Forge strategic partnerships with suppliers, distributors, and industry influencers to expand your reach and access new markets.

171

Collaborate with complementary brands or influencers to co-create content, promotions, or exclusive product offerings.

Invest in Customer Acquisition and Retention:

Implement customer acquisition strategies that target new audiences and drive traffic to your Shopify store.

Focus on customer retention initiatives such as loyalty programs, referral incentives, and personalized communications to maximize customer lifetime value.

Monitor and Analyze Performance Metrics:

Continuously monitor and analyze performance metrics such as conversion rates, average order value (AOV), customer acquisition cost (CAC), and customer lifetime value (CLV).

Use data-driven insights to identify trends, opportunities, and areas for improvement, and adjust your strategies accordingly.

Scale Operations Sustainably:

Scale your operations in a sustainable manner that allows you to maintain quality, consistency, and profitability.

Avoid rapid expansion that may strain resources or compromise customer experience, and focus on incremental growth that aligns with your long-term objectives.

Stay Agile and Adaptive:

Remain agile and adaptive in response to changing market dynamics, consumer preferences, and industry trends.

Continuously iterate, experiment, and evolve your strategies to stay ahead of the competition and capitalize on emerging opportunities.

Expanding Product Offerings and Diversifying Revenue Streams

Expanding product offerings and diversifying revenue streams are essential strategies for Shopify store owners seeking to generate traffic, increase sales, and build a resilient ecommerce business. By

173

broadening the range of products available and exploring new avenues for revenue generation, merchants can capture a larger market share, attract diverse customer segments, and mitigate risks associated with relying on a single product or sales channel. Here's how to expand product offerings and diversify revenue streams on Shopify:

Conduct Market Research:

Conduct thorough market research to identify emerging trends, niche markets, and customer preferences.

Analyze competitor offerings, customer feedback, and industry insights to uncover opportunities for product expansion and diversification.

Identify Complementary Products:

Identify complementary products that align with your existing offerings and cater to the needs and interests of your target audience.

Consider related accessories, add-ons, or variations that enhance the value proposition of your core products.

174

Explore New Product Categories:

Explore new product categories that resonate with your target market and complement your brand identity and values.

Consider expanding into adjacent markets or verticals that present growth opportunities and align with your expertise and resources.

Source Quality Suppliers and Manufacturers:

Identify reputable suppliers, manufacturers, or wholesalers that can provide high-quality products at competitive prices.

Establish strong partnerships and negotiate favorable terms to ensure reliable supply chains and consistent product availability.

Curate Exclusive or Unique Products:

Curate exclusive or unique products that differentiate your Shopify store from competitors and capture the interest of discerning customers.

175

Offer limited edition releases, customizations, or collaborations with designers and artisans to create a sense of exclusivity and scarcity.

Introduce Private Label or White Label Products:

Introduce private label or white label products that bear your brand name and identity, allowing you to control quality, pricing, and branding.

Work with manufacturers to develop custom formulations, packaging, or designs that reflect your brand aesthetics and values.

Create Bundles and Product Kits:

Create product bundles or kits that combine complementary items and offer value-added solutions to customers.

Bundle related products together at a discounted price to encourage upsells and increase average order value (AOV).

176

Launch Digital Products or Services:

Explore opportunities to offer digital products or services that complement your physical offerings and cater to customer needs.

Consider offering ebooks, online courses, consulting services, or digital downloads that provide additional value to your audience.

Explore Subscription Models:

Introduce subscription-based models that offer recurring revenue streams and encourage customer loyalty and retention.

Offer subscription boxes, membership programs, or auto-renewal options for consumable products or curated experiences.

Diversify Sales Channels:

Diversify your sales channels beyond your Shopify store to reach new audiences and markets.

Explore selling on third-party marketplaces, social media platforms, or brick-and-mortar retail locations to expand your reach and distribution network.

177

Monitor Performance and Adapt:

Monitor the performance of new product offerings and revenue streams using analytics and sales data.

Evaluate profitability, customer feedback, and market trends to refine your product assortment and strategic focus over time.

Scaling Marketing Efforts and Reaching New Markets

Scaling marketing efforts and reaching new markets are pivotal strategies for Shopify store owners aiming to generate traffic, increase sales, and expand their customer base. By implementing scalable marketing tactics and exploring untapped market segments, merchants can unlock new growth opportunities and drive sustainable revenue growth. Here's how to scale marketing efforts and reach new markets on Shopify:

Define Target Markets and Segments:

Conduct market research to identify potential target markets and customer segments that align with your products, brand, and value proposition.

Segment your audience based on demographics, psychographics, behavior, and geographic location to tailor marketing messages and strategies effectively.

Develop a Comprehensive Marketing Plan:

Develop a comprehensive marketing plan that outlines goals, strategies, tactics, and key performance indicators (KPIs) for reaching new markets and scaling marketing efforts.

Identify the most effective marketing channels, platforms, and campaigns for reaching your target audience and achieving your business objectives.

Invest in Content Marketing:

Invest in content marketing initiatives such as blogging, video marketing, and content creation to educate, engage, and attract potential customers.

Create valuable, informative content that addresses customer pain points, solves problems, and provides insights relevant to your target market.

179

Optimize for Search Engines (SEO):

Optimize your Shopify store and content for search engines to improve visibility, organic traffic, and search engine rankings.

Conduct keyword research, optimize product descriptions, meta tags, and headings, and build high-quality backlinks to increase your website's authority and relevance.

Utilize Paid Advertising:

Utilize paid advertising channels such as Google Ads, Facebook Ads, Instagram Ads, and other pay-per-click (PPC) platforms to reach new audiences and drive targeted traffic to your Shopify store.

Set clear objectives, define target audiences, and optimize ad campaigns for maximum reach, engagement, and conversion.

Expand Social Media Presence:

Expand your presence on social media platforms such as Facebook, Instagram, Twitter, LinkedIn, and Pinterest to reach new markets and engage with potential customers.

Create compelling content, run targeted ads, and leverage influencer partnerships to amplify your brand message and attract followers.

Explore Influencer Marketing:

Collaborate with influencers, bloggers, and industry experts in your niche to expand your reach and gain credibility among new audiences.

Identify influencers whose values, audience demographics, and interests align with your brand and products, and negotiate mutually beneficial partnerships.

Engage in Email Marketing:

Engage in email marketing campaigns to nurture leads, build relationships, and drive conversions among new and existing customers.

Segment email lists, personalize messages, and deliver valuable content, promotions, and product recommendations to subscribers based on their preferences and behavior.

Optimize User Experience (UX):

Optimize the user experience of your Shopify store to enhance engagement, conversion rates, and customer satisfaction.

Ensure that your website is mobile-friendly, easy to navigate, and optimized for fast loading speeds to provide a seamless browsing and shopping experience.

Monitor, Analyze, and Iterate:

Monitor the performance of your marketing efforts using analytics tools and tracking metrics such as website traffic, conversion rates, click-through rates, and return on investment (ROI).

Analyze data insights to identify trends, opportunities, and areas for improvement, and iterate your marketing strategies accordingly.

Streamlining Operations and Optimizing Fulfillment Processes

Streamlining operations and optimizing fulfillment processes are critical components of managing a successful Shopify store. Efficient operations and streamlined fulfillment workflows not only improve customer satisfaction but also contribute to increased sales, reduced costs, and sustainable growth. Here are key strategies for streamlining operations and optimizing fulfillment processes:

Evaluate Current Processes:

Conduct a comprehensive assessment of your current operational workflows and fulfillment processes.

Identify pain points, bottlenecks, and inefficiencies that may be hindering productivity and customer satisfaction.

Invest in Automation Tools:

Invest in automation tools and software solutions that streamline repetitive tasks and automate manual processes.

Implement order management systems, inventory management software, and shipping solutions that integrate seamlessly with your Shopify store.

Integrate with Third-Party Apps and Services:

Explore third-party integrations and apps available in the Shopify App Store to extend the functionality of your store and streamline operations.

183

Integrate with accounting software, customer relationship management (CRM) systems, and shipping carriers to streamline data management and communication.

Optimize Inventory Management:

Implement inventory management best practices to ensure accurate stock levels, reduce stockouts, and prevent overstocking.

Use inventory tracking tools to monitor stock levels in real-time, set reorder points, and automate replenishment processes.

Implement Just-In-Time (JIT) Inventory Practices:

Adopt just-in-time inventory practices to minimize inventory holding costs and improve cash flow.

Source products and raw materials as needed based on customer demand forecasts and sales trends.

184

Standardize Packaging and Shipping Processes:

Standardize packaging materials, dimensions, and shipping methods to streamline fulfillment operations and reduce shipping costs.

Implement efficient packing procedures to minimize handling time and ensure products are shipped securely and accurately.

Optimize Order Processing Workflows:

Streamline order processing workflows to reduce manual errors and improve order accuracy and efficiency.

Implement standardized order processing procedures and utilize order management software to track orders from receipt to fulfillment.

Offer Multiple Shipping Options:

Offer customers multiple shipping options, including standard, expedited, and same-day delivery, to cater to diverse preferences and delivery needs.

Negotiate competitive shipping rates with carriers and pass on savings to customers through discounted shipping promotions.

Implement Lean Principles:

Apply lean principles such as continuous improvement and waste reduction to optimize operational efficiency and eliminate non-value-added activities.

Implement lean methodologies such as 5S, Kanban, and Kaizen to streamline workflows and drive productivity gains.

Train and Empower Staff:

Provide comprehensive training and resources to staff members involved in fulfillment and operations roles.

Empower employees to take ownership of their roles, identify process improvements, and contribute to operational excellence.

Monitor Performance Metrics:

Monitor key performance metrics such as order cycle time, order accuracy, on-time delivery, and fulfillment costs.

Use performance data to identify areas for improvement, track progress, and measure the impact of optimization efforts.

Staying Updated with Industry Trends and Technology Advancements

In the rapidly evolving landscape of ecommerce, staying updated with industry trends and technology advancements is crucial for Shopify store owners looking to generate traffic, increase sales, and maintain a competitive edge. By keeping abreast of the latest developments and innovations, merchants can identify emerging opportunities, anticipate shifts in consumer behavior, and adapt their strategies to capitalize on evolving market trends. Here are key strategies for staying updated with industry trends and technology advancements:

Attend Industry Conferences and Events:

Participate in industry conferences, trade shows, and networking events to connect with peers, industry experts, and thought leaders.

Attend keynote sessions, workshops, and panel discussions to gain insights into

187

emerging trends, best practices, and future developments in ecommerce.

Join Professional Associations and Communities:

Join professional associations, online forums, and community groups dedicated to ecommerce and digital marketing.

Engage in discussions, share knowledge, and exchange ideas with fellow merchants, experts, and practitioners in the field.

Follow Industry Publications and Blogs:

Follow industry publications, blogs, and online resources that cover topics related to ecommerce, retail trends, and technology advancements.

Subscribe to newsletters, podcasts, and webinars to receive timely updates, analysis, and insights from industry experts.

Monitor Social Media Channels:

Follow relevant influencers, thought leaders, and industry insiders on social media platforms such as Twitter, LinkedIn, and Facebook.

Stay updated with trending topics, news updates, and discussions related to ecommerce, digital marketing, and technology innovations.

Subscribe to Industry Reports and Research Studies:

Subscribe to industry reports, research studies, and market analyses published by reputable research firms and consultancy agencies.

Gain access to valuable data, trends, and forecasts that can inform strategic decision-making and business planning.

Engage with Shopify Updates and Resources:

Stay informed about new features, updates, and enhancements introduced by Shopify through official announcements, blog posts, and developer documentation.

Explore Shopify Academy, webinars, and educational resources to deepen your understanding of ecommerce strategies, tools, and best practices.

189

Experiment with Beta Features and Early Access Programs:

Participate in beta testing programs and early access initiatives offered by Shopify and third-party developers to explore new features and technologies before they are widely released.

Provide feedback, report bugs, and share insights to help shape the future direction of Shopify's platform and ecosystem.

Invest in Continuous Learning and Professional Development:

Invest in continuous learning and professional development opportunities to enhance your skills and expertise in ecommerce, digital marketing, and technology.

Enroll in online courses, workshops, and certification programs offered by reputable institutions and training providers.

Network and Collaborate with Industry Experts:

Build relationships and network with industry experts, consultants, and solution providers who can offer valuable insights, guidance, and support.

190

Seek mentorship, advice, and collaboration opportunities to accelerate your learning and growth as a Shopify store owner.

Monitor Competitor Activity and Market Trends:

Monitor competitor activity, market trends, and consumer behavior to identify opportunities and threats in the competitive landscape.

Conduct regular competitor analysis and market research to benchmark your performance, identify gaps, and differentiate your offerings.

191

CHAPTER 9

CONCLUSION:

EMPOWERING YOUR SHOPIFY JOURNEY

In the dynamic world of ecommerce, mastering the art of generating traffic and increasing sales is the cornerstone of success for Shopify store owners. Throughout this book, we've explored a multitude of strategies, techniques, and best practices designed to empower your Shopify journey and propel your business to new heights.

From understanding your audience and conducting market research to optimizing your store for search engines and leveraging social media marketing, each chapter has provided invaluable insights and actionable steps to help you attract visitors, convert leads, and drive revenue growth.

We've delved into the importance of personalization, the power of content marketing, and the significance of customer engagement in building lasting relationships and fostering brand loyalty. We've discussed the role of data-driven decision-making, the impact of user experience, and the value of continuous learning and adaptation in staying ahead of the competition.

As you navigate the ever-evolving landscape of ecommerce, it's essential to remain agile, innovative, and customer-centric in your approach. Embrace change, experiment with new ideas, and embrace failure as an opportunity to learn and grow. Remember that success in ecommerce is not just about generating sales—it's about creating memorable experiences, delivering value, and building meaningful connections with your audience.

As you embark on your Shopify journey, remember that you are not alone. The Shopify community is a vibrant ecosystem of entrepreneurs, developers, and industry experts who are eager to share knowledge, support one another, and celebrate successes together. Take advantage of the resources, tools, and networks available to you, and don't hesitate to reach out for help and guidance along the way.

193

In closing, remember that your Shopify store is more than just a platform for selling products it's a gateway to endless possibilities, a canvas for creativity, and a vehicle for realizing your entrepreneurial dreams. With dedication, perseverance, and a commitment to excellence, there's no limit to what you can achieve.

Thank you for embarking on this journey with us. Here's to your continued success, growth, and fulfillment as a Shopify entrepreneur.

Recap: Key Strategies for Generating Traffic and Increasing Sales on Shopify

Throughout this book, we've explored a plethora of strategies designed to help Shopify store owners effectively generate traffic and increase sales. Let's recap some of the key strategies highlighted in our journey:

Understanding Your Audience:

Conduct thorough market research to understand your target audience's demographics, preferences, and behaviors.

Tailor your marketing messages, product offerings, and user experience to resonate with your audience's needs and interests.

Optimizing Your Shopify Store:

Design an attractive, user-friendly website that provides a seamless browsing and shopping experience across devices.

Optimize product listings for search engines (SEO) to improve visibility and attract organic traffic to your store.

Content Marketing Strategies:

Create valuable, engaging content that educates, entertains, and inspires your audience.

Leverage blogging, video marketing, and social media content to establish thought leadership and build brand authority.

Social Media Marketing:

Identify the most effective social media platforms for your audience and engage with them through compelling content and interactions.

Utilize social media advertising, influencer partnerships, and user-generated content to expand your reach and drive engagement.

Email Marketing Campaigns:

Build and nurture relationships with your audience through targeted email marketing campaigns.

Segment your email list, personalize your messages, and provide exclusive offers and incentives to encourage conversions.

Search Engine Marketing (SEM) and Pay-Per-Click (PPC) Advertising:

Implement SEM and PPC campaigns to drive targeted traffic to your Shopify store.

Conduct keyword research, create compelling ad copy, and optimize landing pages to maximize ad performance and ROI.

Leveraging Analytics and Data Insights:

Utilize analytics tools to track website traffic, user behavior, and conversion rates.

Analyze data insights to identify trends, optimize marketing strategies, and make data-driven decisions to improve performance.

196

Enhancing Customer Experience:

Provide exceptional customer service and support to build trust and loyalty among your audience.

Implement responsive design, effective product categorization, and intuitive navigation to enhance the shopping experience.

Expanding Product Offerings and Diversifying Revenue Streams:

Expand your product catalog to cater to diverse customer needs and preferences.

Diversify revenue streams through subscription services, digital products, and strategic partnerships.

Staying Updated with Industry Trends and Technology Advancements:

Stay abreast of industry trends, technology advancements, and best practices in ecommerce.

Engage in continuous learning, networking, and experimentation to stay ahead of the curve and capitalize on emerging opportunities.

197

Encouragement: Embrace Continuous Learning and Adaptation

In the ever-evolving landscape of e-commerce, embracing continuous learning and adaptation is not just a choice it's a necessity for thriving in a dynamic and competitive environment. As Shopify store owners, you are at the forefront of innovation, entrepreneurship, and digital commerce. Your journey is marked by endless opportunities, challenges, and moments of growth. Here's why continuous learning and adaptation are essential for your success:

Stay Ahead of the Curve:

The e-commerce landscape is constantly evolving, driven by technological advancements, changing consumer behavior, and market trends. By committing to continuous learning, you can stay ahead of the curve and anticipate shifts in the industry before they happen.

Embrace Innovation and Experimentation:

Innovation is the lifeblood of e-commerce. By continuously learning about emerging technologies, marketing strategies, and customer preferences, you can innovate and experiment with new ideas to drive growth and differentiate your Shopify store.

Adapt to Changing Consumer Needs:

Consumer needs and preferences are constantly evolving. By staying informed about market trends and customer insights, you can adapt your products, services, and marketing strategies to meet the changing demands of your audience.

Remain Agile and Responsive:

In today's fast-paced digital world, agility is key to success. By cultivating a culture of continuous learning and adaptation within your organization, you can respond quickly to market shifts, capitalize on opportunities, and mitigate risks.

Challenge Yourself to Grow:

Continuous learning is not just about acquiring new skills—it's about challenging

199

yourself to grow, both personally and professionally. By stepping out of your comfort zone, experimenting with new ideas, and embracing failure as a learning opportunity, you can unlock your full potential as an entrepreneur.

Build Resilience and Tenacity:

The journey of entrepreneurship is filled with ups and downs, setbacks, and triumphs. By embracing continuous learning and adaptation, you can build resilience, tenacity, and the ability to navigate challenges with grace and determination.

Forge Connections and Collaborations:

Learning is not a solitary pursuit it's a collaborative endeavor. By engaging with peers, mentors, industry experts, and the Shopify community, you can exchange ideas, share insights, and forge meaningful connections that propel your growth and success.

Inspire Innovation and Creativity:

Continuous learning fuels innovation and creativity. By exposing yourself to diverse perspectives, disciplines, and experiences, you can spark new ideas, challenge conventional thinking, and push the boundaries of what's possible in e-commerce.

Lead with Purpose and Vision:

As a Shopify store owner, you are not just a business owner—you are a visionary leader with the power to inspire change and make a meaningful impact. By embodying a spirit of continuous learning and adaptation, you can lead with purpose, vision, and a commitment to excellence.

Celebrate Progress and Milestones:

Celebrate every milestone, achievement, and breakthrough along your journey of continuous learning and adaptation. Each step forward is a testament to your resilience, dedication, and unwavering commitment to growth.

Final Thoughts and Encouragement for Success in Shopify Entrepreneurship

As we conclude our journey through the pages of "Shopify: Generating Traffic and Increasing Sales," I want to leave you with some final thoughts and words of encouragement for your success in Shopify entrepreneurship.

Embarking on the path of entrepreneurship is an exhilarating adventure filled with challenges, triumphs, and countless opportunities for growth. Your decision to build and grow a Shopify store signifies not just a business venture, but a journey of self-discovery, innovation, and resilience.

As you navigate the complexities of the e-commerce landscape, remember these key principles:

Passion and Purpose: Your passion for your products and your vision for your brand are the driving forces behind your Shopify journey. Stay true to your values, your mission, and your purpose as you build your business.

Perseverance and Resilience:
Entrepreneurship is not for the faint of heart. Embrace challenges as opportunities for growth, setbacks as lessons in resilience, and failures as stepping stones toward success. Keep moving forward, even in the face of adversity.

Continuous Learning and Adaptation: The e-commerce landscape is ever-evolving, and success belongs to those who are willing to learn, adapt, and innovate. Stay curious, stay hungry for knowledge, and never stop seeking new ways to improve and grow.

Customer-Centric Focus: Your customers are at the heart of your business. Listen to their needs, understand their pain points, and strive to exceed their expectations at every touchpoint. Build meaningful connections, foster trust, and prioritize the customer experience above all else.

Community and Collaboration:
You are not alone on this journey. The Shopify community is a vibrant ecosystem of entrepreneurs, developers, and experts

who are here to support you, inspire you, and celebrate your successes. Embrace collaboration, seek mentorship, and pay it forward to others along the way.

Vision and Innovation: Dare to dream big, think outside the box, and challenge the status quo. Innovation is the lifeblood of entrepreneurship, and visionary leaders have the power to shape the future of commerce. Let your imagination soar, and never be afraid to pursue bold ideas that set you apart.

Gratitude and Celebration: Celebrate every milestone, no matter how small. Take time to reflect on how far you've come, acknowledge your achievements, and express gratitude for the journey. Success is not just about reaching the destination it's about embracing the journey and the lessons learned along the way.

As you embark on your Shopify entrepreneurship journey, remember that success is not defined by the destination, but by the growth, impact, and fulfillment you experience along the way. Embrace the challenges, cherish the victories, and savor every moment of the adventure.

May your Shopify store be a beacon of innovation, a haven of inspiration, and a catalyst for positive change in the world of e-commerce. Believe in yourself, trust in your vision, and never underestimate the power of your dreams to transform the world.